Contents

Part 1:	Introduction	2
	About the plays	2
	Phonic knowledge	2
	Introducing the plays	4
	Selecting the right part for each child	5
	Plays resources	6
Part 2:	Folk tales plays	8
	How the Zebras Got Their Stripes	8
	Why Anansi the Spider has Eight Thin Legs	14
Part 3:	Inky Mouse investigates plays	20
	Detective Inky in... The Case of the Golden Trainer	20
	Detective Inky in... The Case of the Vanishing Cakes	26
Part 4:	Discoveries plays	32
	The Un-Lucky Ring	32
	The Rainbow	38
Part 5:	Using the plays	44
	Comprehension and discussion questions	46
	Songs	52
	Story sequencing	58
	Comic strip templates	64
	Looking at the characters	66
	Cross-curricular activities	72
	Mask and prop templates	78

Part 1: Introduction

About the plays

This book contains six plays, which have been written specifically to help children develop their reading fluency and their communication skills. The plays in this book do not have to be performed; they work equally well when used for group, guided or individual reading. Whether the children perform or simply read the plays aloud, they will be getting valuable reading, speaking and listening practice. A number of accompanying comprehension questions, discussion topics, cross-curricular activities and writing activities have been included for each play to reinforce this learning.

Although performance is not necessary, all of the plays have been designed to be as simple to produce as possible. Only one of the plays requires a raised stage platform, and the prop and costume requirements have been deliberately kept to a minimum, with any specific masks or props provided as templates within this book. There is also a song for each play, so that every child in the class can feel included in the performance, whether they were given a speaking part or not. For those children who were given a speaking part, helpful tips for performing have been included at the end of each play script.

There are three different types of play in this book. The first two plays: *How the Zebras Got Their Stripes* and *Why Anansi the Spider has Eight Thin Legs* are based on widely known African folk tales. Folk tales are stories that are typically passed on orally, without being written down. Often, folk tales try to explain why something in the natural world is the way it is: for example, why a zebra has stripes. There is usually also a moral lesson to be learnt from a folk tale: in *How the Zebras Got Their Stripes,* the baboon's selfishness leads to his losing all of the fur on his bottom. The next two plays are 'whodunnit-style' mysteries, featuring the Jolly Phonics character Inky Mouse as a detective who works together with her friends, Snake and Bee, to solve crimes. The final two plays: *The Un-Lucky Ring* and *The Rainbow* are designed to make the children think about the world around them. *The Un-Lucky Ring* encourages the children to discuss the nature of luck and think about whether success comes as a result of good luck or is earned, while *The Rainbow* helps children to learn about the weather and prompts them to find out about how and why rainbows occur. It is a good idea to read this play alongside the folk tales plays, which attempt to explain why zebras have stripes and why spiders have long, thin legs. The difference between *The Rainbow* and the folk tales plays is that the explanation given for rainbows is a simplified version of scientific fact. The six plays can be used in any order.

Phonic knowledge

All six plays have been written so that the text is fully decodable. The table opposite shows the phonic knowledge required to read the plays. (If the children learnt to read with Jolly Phonics, this phonic knowledge will have been taught by the end of the children's first year, and it is the same as that used in the Jolly Phonics Purple Level readers.)

Letter sounds	Letter-sound spellings
/s/	⟨s⟩, ⟨ss⟩ and soft ⟨c⟩ as in '**s**ack', 'dre**ss**', 'ni**c**e', 'a**c**id' and '**c**y**c**le'
/a/	⟨a⟩ as in '**a**nd'
/t/	⟨t⟩ and ⟨tt⟩ as in '**t**op' and 'bu**tt**on'
/i/	⟨i⟩ as in '**i**ndigo'
/p/	⟨p⟩ and ⟨pp⟩ as in '**p**en' and 'ha**pp**y'
/n/	⟨n⟩ and ⟨nn⟩ as in '**n**et' and 'fu**nn**y'
/ck/	⟨c⟩, ⟨k⟩ and ⟨ck⟩ as in '**c**up', '**k**it' and 'sa**ck**'
/e/	⟨e⟩ as in '**e**nd'
/h/	⟨h⟩ as in '**h**elp'
/r/	⟨r⟩ and ⟨rr⟩ as in '**r**ed' and 'hu**rr**y'
/m/	⟨m⟩ and ⟨mm⟩ as in '**m**ust' and 'tu**mm**y'
/d/	⟨d⟩ and ⟨dd⟩ as in '**d**ig' and 'mu**dd**y'
/g/	⟨g⟩ and ⟨gg⟩ as in '**g**ap' and 'fo**gg**y'
/o/	⟨o⟩ as in '**o**tter'
/u/	⟨u⟩ as in '**u**nder'
/l/	⟨l⟩ and ⟨ll⟩ as in '**l**ast' and 'fri**ll**y'
/f/	⟨f⟩, ⟨ff⟩ and ⟨ph⟩ as in '**f**un', 'scru**ff**y' and 'dol**ph**in'
/b/	⟨b⟩ and ⟨bb⟩ as in '**b**ud' and 'ra**bb**it'
/ai/	⟨ai⟩, ⟨a_e⟩ and ⟨ay⟩ as in '**ai**m', 'm**a**k**e**' and 'pl**ay**'
/j/	⟨j⟩ and soft ⟨g⟩ as in '**j**og', '**g**em', '**g**inger' and 'din**g**y'
/oa/	⟨oa⟩, ⟨o_e⟩ and ⟨ow⟩ as in '**oa**ts', 'st**o**n**e**' and 'sn**ow**'
/ie/	⟨ie⟩, ⟨i_e⟩, ⟨y⟩ and ⟨igh⟩ as in 'l**ie**s', 'l**i**k**e**', 'sk**y**' and 'h**igh**'
/ee/	⟨ee⟩, ⟨y⟩, ⟨e_e⟩ and ⟨ea⟩ as in '**ee**l', 'happ**y**', 'th**e**s**e**' and 't**ea**'
/or/	⟨or⟩, ⟨al⟩, ⟨au⟩, ⟨aw⟩ as in '**or**der', 't**al**k', 'f**au**n' and 'cl**aw**'
/z/	⟨z⟩ and ⟨zz⟩ as in '**z**oo' and 'fu**zz**y'
/w/	⟨w⟩ as in '**w**ent'
/ng/	⟨ng⟩ as in 'so**ng**'
/v/	⟨v⟩ as in '**v**et'
little /oo/	⟨oo⟩ as in 'l**oo**k'
long /oo/	⟨oo⟩ as in 'sp**oo**n' (⟨ue⟩, ⟨u_e⟩ and ⟨ew⟩ as in 'gl**ue**', 'fl**u**t**e**' and 'dr**ew**')
/y/	⟨y⟩ as in '**y**es'
/x/	⟨x⟩ as in 'mi**x**'
/ch/	⟨ch⟩ as in '**ch**op'
/sh/	⟨sh⟩ as in '**sh**ip'
/th/ (voiced)	⟨th⟩ as in '**th**en'
/th/ (unvoiced)	⟨th⟩ as in '**th**in'
/qu/	⟨qu⟩ as in '**qu**ick'
/ou/	⟨ou⟩ and ⟨ow⟩ as in '**ou**tside' and 'c**ow**'
/oi/	⟨oi⟩ and ⟨oy⟩ as in '**oi**l' and 't**oy**'
/ue/	⟨ue⟩, ⟨u_e⟩ and ⟨ew⟩ as in 'val**ue**', 'c**u**t**e**' and 'f**ew**'
/er/	⟨er⟩, ⟨ir⟩ and ⟨ur⟩ as in 'st**er**n', 'b**ir**d' and 't**ur**n'
/ar/	⟨ar⟩ as in '**ar**t'
/air/	⟨air⟩, ⟨ear⟩ and ⟨are⟩ as in 'ch**air**', 'b**ear**' and 'squ**are**'

The children will also need to be able to read the following tricky words, character names and days of the week.

Tricky words						Character names	Days of the week
I	you	one	why	saw	once	Inky	Monday
the	your	by	where	put	upon	Snake	Tuesday
he	come	only	who	could	always	Bee	Wednesday
she	some	old	which	should	also	Anansi	Thursday
me	said	like	any	would	of		Friday
we	here	have	many	right	eight		Saturday
be	there	live	more	two	love		Sunday
was	they	give	before	four	cover		
to	go	little	other	goes	after		
do	no	down	were	does	every		
are	so	what	because	made	mother		
all	my	when	want	their	father		

Introducing the plays

When introducing a play for the first time, it can be helpful to explain what a play is and point out some of the differences between a play script and a storybook. Both a storybook and a play script tell a story, but they look quite different. In a storybook, we are told what the characters do and think in the same section of text, and anything the characters say is put inside speech marks. A play, on the other hand, looks like a conversation written down. If the characters do anything while speaking, this is explained in short stage directions. Sometimes, a play has a narrator, too. The narrator is like another character who helps us to understand what is happening in the play. All of these differences are because a play is meant to be acted out as well as read, whereas a storybook is only meant to be read. It can be helpful to show the children the two text examples below and opposite, and help them to spot the main features of each type of text.

Storybook text looks like this:

> Megan has been studying hard all day because she has an important maths test tomorrow. Tom also has a test on Monday. His is a spelling test, but he has not been studying quite as hard as Megan. While Megan practised her maths, Tom sat with his head on the desk and snored loudly.
>
> After a little while, Dad came in and said, "Megan, you've been studying for hours now. You should have a rest. Why not come for a walk in the woods with me?"
>
> When Dad suggested a walk, Tom woke up with a start and said, "What's that? A walk? What a good plan! I'll go and get Mum."

A play script looks like this:

> **Narrator 1:** Megan has been studying hard all day because she has an important maths test tomorrow.
>
> **Narrator 2:** Tom also has a test on Monday. His is a spelling test, but he has not been studying quite as hard as Megan.
>
> **Megan:** Two times two is four; two times three is six; two times four is eight...
>
> *Tom sits with his head on the desk and snores loudly.*
>
> **Dad:** Megan, you've been studying for hours now. You should have a rest. Why not come for a walk in the woods with me?
>
> **Tom:** (Wakes up with a start) What's that? A walk? What a good plan! I'll go and get Mum.

Selecting the right part for each child

Selecting the right part for each child is important. Each part has been colour-coded according to difficulty level and length, so that teachers can allocate an appropriate part to each child.

Difficult or long parts — Parts labelled **red** should only be given to confident fluent readers, with good, up-to-date phonic knowledge. These parts will be long and will have a number of alternative letter-sound spellings.

Parts of average length and difficulty — Parts labelled **amber** can be given to good-to-average readers, who know most of the alternative letter-sound spellings that have been taught. These parts will be shorter than parts labelled red and will contain fewer alternative letter-sound spellings.

Short, simple parts — Parts labelled **green** can be given to less able readers and less confident children. These parts will typically be only one or two lines long and will contain few, or no, alternative spellings.

In some of the plays, there are also non-speaking parts. Once you have allocated all of the parts, provide a copy of the play for each child and encourage them to read through the whole play and highlight their lines. If performing the plays, the children can take their copies of the play home to practise their lines with their parents. It is important to reassure the children that they do not need to learn their lines perfectly; they just need to be able to convey the plot of the play to the audience.

Plays resources

The following resources are included for each play.

A play script
All of the play scripts in this book are reproducible. Make sure that every child has a copy of the play.

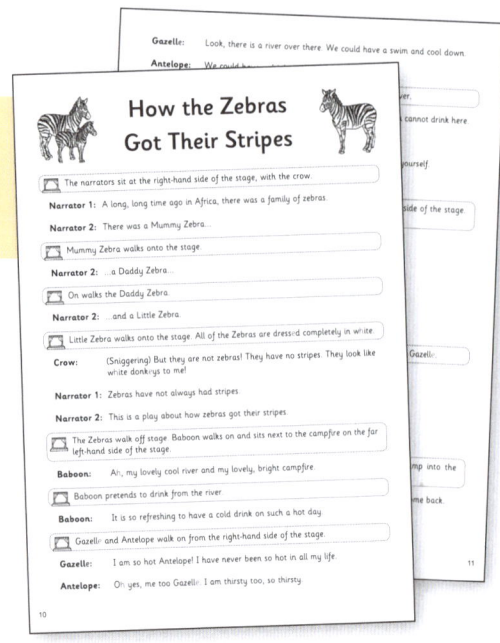

Mask and prop templates
Reproducible animal masks and prop templates are provided for all of the plays. Instructions for making any additional props are also included.

Song lyrics
There is one song for each of the plays. The songs can be used whether the children are performing the plays or not. To download the songs audio, visit **jollylearning.co.uk/login**; log in or register; go to **My resources**; and enter the code: **JPLAYSBE1**.

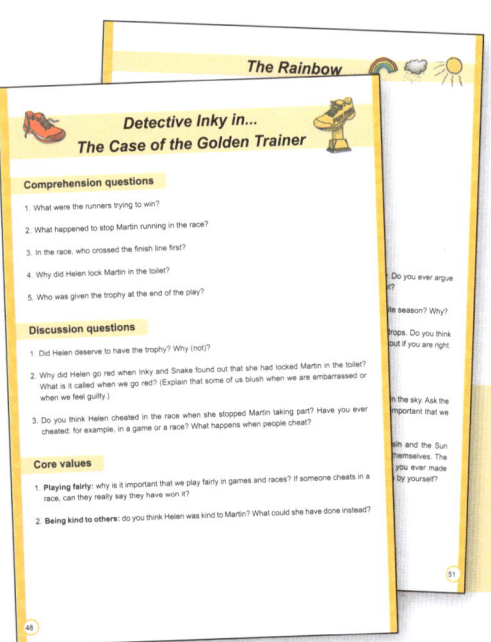

Comprehension and discussion questions
Comprehension and discussion questions encourage the children to recall and think deeply about what they have read. There is a set of such questions for each play.

Story sequencing

There is a reproducible story sequencing activity for each of the plays. Use these to improve the children's reading comprehension skills.

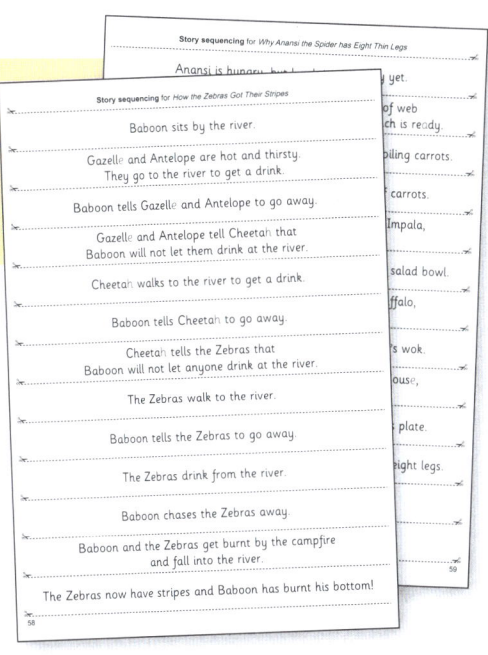

Comic strip templates

Use these reproducible comic strip templates to help the children to retell the play stories in picture form.

Activity pages

Further improve the children's reading comprehension with these reproducible activity pages. There is one activity page for each play.

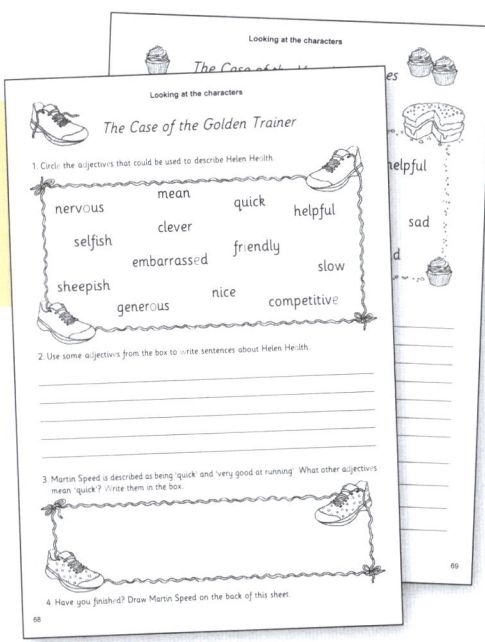

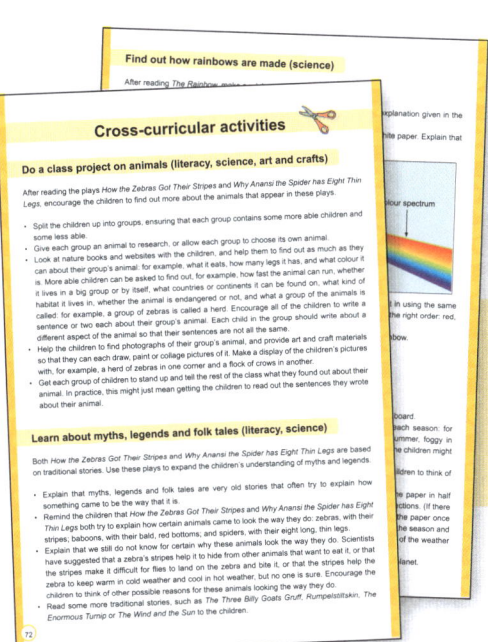

Cross-curricular activity suggestions

Suggestions for art, crafts, science, physical education and cooking activities are also included for cross-curricular learning.

Use some, or all, of these resources when reading or performing the plays.

Part 2: Folk tales plays

How the Zebras Got Their Stripes

This play has ten speaking parts. If you are using this play for group or guided reading, simply allocate the parts and provide one copy of the play for each child. (See pages 10 to 13 for a reproducible play script.) If you are intending to perform the play, the following pages provide suggested costumes for each character and outline the props necessary for performing the play.

Characters

- Narrator 1
- Narrator 2
- Baboon

- Daddy Zebra
- Little Zebra
- Crow
- Gazelle
- Antelope
- Cheetah

- Mummy Zebra

A teacher could read the narrators' parts if necessary. A teacher could also read the stage directions if the play is being used for group or guided reading.

Costume suggestions

Narrator 1 and Narrator 2
These children could either dress as African animals, or they could wear their usual school clothes.

Baboon
This child should wear brown clothes and a baboon mask. (See page 79 for the mask template.)

Crow
This child should wear black clothes and, if possible, black wings. He or she should also wear a crow mask. (See page 80 for the mask template.)

Mummy Zebra, Daddy Zebra and Little Zebra
These children should wear white clothes and white 'donkey' masks at first (see page 81 for the mask template). They should also have zebra masks (see page 82 for the mask template) and black and white striped tops prepared for later in the play.

Gazelle and Antelope
These children should wear light brown clothes and a gazelle or antelope mask. (See page 83 and 84 for the mask templates.)

8

Cheetah
This child should wear yellow or, if possible, cheetah print clothes and a cheetah mask. (See page 85 for the mask template.)

You will need...

A simple stage or stage area
For this play, a raised stage is not necessary; an area of free floor space will also work well.

Animal masks
Make up the various animal masks by using the templates provided and following the instructions on page 78. Note that the zebra mask and the white 'donkey' mask will both need to be photocopied three times, so that each zebra has both a plain white zebra mask for the beginning of the play, and a striped zebra mask for the end of the play.

A campfire
Photocopy the flames templates provided on pages 98 and 99. Stick the flames onto some thick card and paint them white, yellow, orange and red. When dry, cut out the flames and slot them together so that they stand up. Stick on some red, yellow and orange tissue paper; then glue some twigs around the base of the flames to form a little campfire.

Sun, waterfall and tree pictures
Cut out a large disc from yellow paper for the sun. On some very large pieces of paper, paint a waterfall and several trees, and cut them out.

Stage setting

Set the stage to look like an African savannah. Fix a large paper sun and a large picture of a waterfall to the wall behind the left-hand side of the stage. Add some tree pictures to the wall around the waterfall to form a little oasis. The area in front of the waterfall picture will act as the river. Place the campfire on the far left-hand side of the stage, next to the river. The narrators sit at the right-hand side of the stage, accompanied by the crow.

Song

Any children who were not given a speaking part can be encouraged to sing the song 'The Mean Baboon' at the end of the play. Reproducible song lyrics are provided on page 52, and an audio track is available from the Jolly Learning website. Visit **jollylearning.co.uk/login**; log in or register; go to **My resources**; and enter the code: **JPLAYSBE1**.

How the Zebras Got Their Stripes

> The narrators sit at the right-hand side of the stage, with the crow.

Narrator 1: A long, long time ago in Africa, there was a family of zebras.

Narrator 2: There was a Mummy Zebra...

> Mummy Zebra walks onto the stage.

Narrator 2: ...a Daddy Zebra...

> On walks the Daddy Zebra.

Narrator 2: ...and a Little Zebra.

> Little Zebra walks onto the stage. All of the Zebras are dressed completely in white.

Crow: (Sniggering) But they are not zebras! They have no stripes. They look like white donkeys to me!

Narrator 1: Zebras have not always had stripes.

Narrator 2: This is a play about how zebras got their stripes.

> The Zebras walk off stage. Baboon walks on and sits next to the campfire on the far left-hand side of the stage.

Baboon: Ah, my lovely cool river and my lovely, bright campfire.

> Baboon pretends to drink from the river.

Baboon: It is so refreshing to have a cold drink on such a hot day.

> Gazelle and Antelope walk on from the right-hand side of the stage.

Gazelle: I am so hot Antelope! I have never been so hot in all my life.

Antelope: Oh yes, me too Gazelle. I am thirsty too, so thirsty.

Gazelle: Look, there is a river over there. We could have a swim and cool down.

Antelope: We could have a drink, too.

> Gazelle and Antelope walk across the stage to drink from the river.

Baboon: What do you think you are doing? This is my river! You cannot drink here.

Gazelle: You cannot own a river. It is for everyone.

Antelope: (Nodding) Yes, it is very selfish to keep the river all to yourself.

Baboon: (Shouting) GET AWAY FROM MY RIVER!

> Antelope and Gazelle yelp and run away towards the right-hand side of the stage. They almost bump into Cheetah.

Cheetah: Why are you running?

Antelope: Baboon shouted at us.

Gazelle: He said that we could not drink from the river.

Antelope: He says that the river belongs to him.

Cheetah: Nonsense! He doesn't own the river. I'll show him.

> Cheetah heads off to drink from the river, followed by Antelope and Gazelle.

Crow: That is one brave Cheetah!

Baboon: (To Cheetah) Get away from my river.

Cheetah: I just want a little drink.

Baboon: (Shouting) GET AWAY FROM MY RIVER!

> Cheetah, Antelope and Gazelle yelp and run away. They almost bump into the Zebras, who walk onto the stage from the right-hand side.

Crow: (To the audience) I was wondering when the Zebras would come back.

Mummy Zebra: (To Antelope, Gazelle and Cheetah) What's wrong?

Daddy Zebra: What are you running away from?

Cheetah: (To the Zebras) Baboon will not let us drink from the river. He says it is just for him.

Daddy Zebra: He cannot own the river.

Mummy Zebra: He sounds like a very grumpy, selfish Baboon to me.

Little Zebra: We'll show him!

> The Zebras all walk across the stage to the river and Baboon.

Little Zebra: The river is for all of us, not just you, Baboon.

Baboon: Get away from my river! It is mine – all mine!

Daddy Zebra: (To Baboon) You shouldn't be so grumpy and selfish.

> The Zebras all bend down and pretend to drink from the river.

Baboon: (Looking angrily at the Zebras) Grrrrr! I am really angry now.

Crow: Look out, Zebras!

> Baboon runs at the Zebras, and they all run around the campfire – while pretending to fall into it – and then jump into the river.

All: SPLASH!

Baboon and Zebras: Aaaah! Ow! Ouch!

> The Zebras gallop straight across the river and off the stage, but the Baboon stays on stage, sitting in the river, waving his arms and pretending to struggle. While off-stage, the Zebras put on their striped zebra costumes.

Baboon: Help! Help me! I'm drowning!

Cheetah: (To Antelope and Gazelle) We should go and help him.

> Antelope, Gazelle and Cheetah rescue Baboon from the river.

Baboon: Ow! Ow, my bottom! I burnt my bottom on the campfire as I fell, and now all the fur has come off! Ow-ee!

Cheetah: It serves you right for being so grumpy and selfish.

Crow: But what happened to the Zebras?

> The Zebras walk back on stage wearing their black and white striped costumes.

Cheetah, Gazelle and Antelope: Zebras! What happened?

Daddy Zebra: The flames scorched our fur as we fell into the campfire.

Little Zebra: And now we all have black and white stripes!

Daddy Zebra: (To Baboon) Your bottom looks a bit red, Baboon. Did you burn it on your campfire?

Baboon: Yes! It hurts, and all the fur has come off!

Daddy Zebra: I hope you have learnt a lesson, Baboon.

Baboon: Yes, I have. I shall never be so selfish again.

Cheetah, Antelope and Gazelle: At least now we can all have a drink from the river.

All: Hooray!

Narrator 1: So that is how the Zebras got their stripes.

Crow: And how Baboon lost all the fur on his bottom!

THE END

Tips for performing
- Speak slowly and clearly.
- Do not worry if you forget a line or make a mistake.
- Enjoy it!

Why Anansi the Spider has Eight Thin Legs

This play has twelve speaking parts. If you are using this play for group or guided reading, simply allocate the parts and provide one copy of the play for each child. (See pages 16 to 19 for a reproducible play script.) If you are intending to perform the play, the following pages provide suggested costumes for each character and outline the props necessary for performing the play.

Characters

- Narrator 1
- Narrator 2
- Anansi

- Mummy Spider
- Rabbit
- Chimp
- Impala
- Frog
- Mouse
- Lizard

- Crow
- Buffalo

A teacher could read the narrators' parts if necessary. A teacher could also read the stage directions if the play is being used for group or guided reading.

Costume suggestions

Narrator 1 and Narrator 2
These children could either dress up as African animals, or they could wear their usual school clothes.

Crow
This child should wear black clothes and, if possible, black wings. He or she should also wear a crow mask. (See page 80 for the mask template.)

Anansi and Mummy Spider
These children should wear spider masks and black clothes, with four black ribbons or strips of fabric, tied to their waists to form four additional legs. (See page 86 for the mask template.)

Rabbit
This child should wear grey, brown, black or white clothes and a matching rabbit mask. (See page 87 for the mask template.)

Chimp and Buffalo
These children should wear brown or black clothes and a chimp or buffalo mask. (See pages 88 and 89 for the mask templates.)

Impala and Mouse
These children should wear light brown clothes and an impala or mouse mask. (See pages 90 and 91 for the mask templates.)

Frog and Lizard
These children should wear green clothes and a frog or lizard mask. (See pages 92 and 93 for the mask templates.)

You will need...

A simple stage or stage area
For this play, a raised stage is not necessary; an area of free floor space will also work well.

Animal masks
Make up the various animal masks by using the templates provided and following the instructions on page 78. Note that the spider mask will need to be copied twice. Find photographs of each of the animals in the play and get the children to colour in their own mask in the right colours.

Kitchenware
Mummy Spider, Rabbit, Chimp, Impala, Frog, Buffalo, Mouse and Lizard will each need a wooden spoon and either a large cooking pot, a saucepan, a wok, a plate or bowl.

House pictures
See page 73 for the 'Looking at different homes' activity. Provide a large sheet of paper for each child in the class. The children each paint a picture of the kind of home they would like to have. The best five of these pictures can then be stuck to the wall behind the stage so as to form a little street.

Stage setting

Set the stage to look like a little street, with five paintings of houses fixed to the wall behind the stage. In front of the house pictures sit (from left to right) Mummy Spider (with a cooking pot), Rabbit (with a saucepan), Impala and Chimp (with salad bowls), Frog and Buffalo (with a wok), and Mouse and Lizard (with a large plate). The two narrators, Crow and Anansi stand or sit by the left-hand side of the stage.

Song

Any children who were not given a speaking part can be encouraged to sing the song 'Anansi the Spider Likes' at the end of the play. Reproducible song lyrics are provided on page 53, and an audio track is available from the Jolly Learning website. Visit **jollylearning.co.uk/login**; log in or register; go to **My resources**; and enter the code: **JPLAYSBE1**.

Why Anansi the Spider has Eight Thin Legs

> The narrators sit at the left-hand side of the stage, with the crow.

Narrator 1: Once upon a time, there was a spider called Anansi. He had eight short legs.

Crow: Short legs? But spiders have long legs...

Narrator 1: Well yes, they do now, but spiders have not always had long legs.

Narrator 2: This play is about how one spider, called Anansi, got his long legs.

> Anansi walks on stage and waves.

Narrator 1: One morning, Anansi was feeling particularly hungry. He said to his mum...

Anansi: Mum, when will lunch be ready? My tummy is rumbling.

Mummy Spider: I have only just started cooking! Why not go for a little walk? Lunch will be ready when you get back.

Anansi: But how will I know when lunch is ready if I am out walking?

Mummy Spider: You can spin a little strand of your web and tie one end to the cooking pot and the other end to one of your legs. When lunch is ready I will tug on the web to let you know.

Anansi: That is an excellent plan!

> Anansi pretends to tie one end of a strand of web to the cooking pot and the other end to his ankle.

Mummy Spider: Enjoy your walk. Remember to come running when I tug on the web.

> Anansi whistles and walks along the stage.

Narrator 2: Anansi walks along, whistling to himself, until he sees...

Anansi: Rabbit! Good morning! What are you doing?

Rabbit: Hello, Anansi! I am boiling carrots for my lunch.

Anansi: Mmmmmm, carrots! May I have some?

Rabbit: They are still quite raw, but they will be cooked soon. Why not stay until they are ready?

Anansi: I have a better plan. I will spin a little strand of my web, and tie one end to the pan and the other end to one of my legs. When the carrots are ready you can tug on the web to let me know.

> Anansi pretends to tie one end of a strand of web to the pan of carrots and the other end to his ankle.

Rabbit: What a clever plan! I'll see you soon, then.

Anansi: Bye, Rabbit!

> Anansi hums and walks along the stage.

Narrator 1: Anansi sets off again, humming to himself, until he sees…

Anansi: Chimp! Impala! Hello! What are you up to?

Impala: I am mixing the salad leaves for our lunch.

Chimp: And I am chopping up the melon and grapes.

Anansi: Melon and grapes are lovely! Can I have some, please?

Impala: The melon and grapes are for after lunch. Why not stay and eat with us?

Anansi: Oh no, I have a better plan. I will spin a strand of web and tie one end to the salad bowl and one end to my leg. When you are ready for the melon and grapes, you can tug on the web to let me know.

Chimp: What a brilliant plan! We'll see you soon.

> Anansi pretends to tie one end of a strand of web to the salad bowl and the other end to his ankle.

Anansi: Bye, Chimp! Bye, Impala! I'll see you soon.
Tra, la, la, la…

> Anansi sings and walks across the stage.

Narrator 2: Anansi sets off again on his walk, singing to himself, until he sees...

Anansi: Frog! Buffalo! Hello! What have you got there?

Frog: I have some peas and cashew nuts that I got at the market.

Buffalo: And I have some mushrooms that I picked this morning.

Anansi: I really love peas and mushrooms. Please can I have some?

Frog: Not yet. We are going to make a stir-fry with them first. Why not stay and help us cook it?

Narrator 1: But Anansi had a better plan. He tied a strand of his web to the wok and said...

Anansi: Just tug on this strand of web when the stir-fry is ready, and I'll come running.

Buffalo: What an excellent plan, Anansi! We'll see you soon.

Narrator 2: So Anansi set off again, grinning to himself, until he saw...

Anansi: Mouse! Lizard! Hello! Is that cheese I can see?

Mouse: Yes, we are having cheese sandwiches for our lunch.

Lizard: I am cutting them into lots of different shapes and putting them on this plate.

Anansi: Wow, they look good! Can I have some?

Mouse: We haven't quite finished yet. Shall we call you when they are ready?

Anansi: No need! I can tie a strand of my web to the plate and you can tug on it to let me know.

Lizard: What a marvellous plan! We'll see you soon.

Anansi: Bye, Lizard! Bye, Mouse! See you soon.

Crow: Anansi is very greedy, isn't he?

Narrator 2: Yes, he is.

Narrator 1: Before long, Anansi had a strand of web tied to each of his eight legs. He set off again on his walk, beaming to himself, and thinking about all of the lovely food awaiting him...

Narrator 2: When suddenly, all of the food was ready at once!

> All of the children playing Anansi's friends pretend to tug on the strands of web that are tied to Anansi's legs. Anansi stretches out his arms and legs.

Anansi: Help! All of my legs are being tugged at once! Ouch! Help! My legs are stretching! Ow-ee!

> Anansi stands in the middle of the stage, with arms and legs outstretched.

All: TWANG!

> Anansi shakes his arms and legs.

Anansi: Oh, thank goodness! All of the strands of web have snapped.

> All of the other characters come running up to help Anansi.

Frog: What happened?

Chimp: We heard you shouting.

Anansi: All of you tugged on the webs at once!

Mouse: Anansi, look at your legs! They were all short and stubby before, but now they are long and thin.

Mummy Spider: So they are!

Anansi: Sniff, sniff. They are very sore.

Narrator 1: So that is how Anansi got his long, thin legs

Crow: All of his legs got stretched! Ouch!

THE END

Tips for performing
- Speak slowly and clearly.
- Do not worry if you forget a line or make a mistake.
- Enjoy it!

Part 3: Inky Mouse investigates plays

Detective Inky in... The Case of the Golden Trainer

This play has thirteen speaking parts. If you are using this play for group or guided reading, simply allocate the parts and provide one copy of the play for each child. (See pages 22 to 25 for a reproducible play script.) If you are intending to perform the play, the following pages provide suggested costumes for each character and outline the props necessary for performing the play.

Characters

- Narrator
- Inky
- Fun Run Organiser

- Snake
- Fun Run Helper
- Martin Speed
- Helen Health
- Jimmy Quick

- Bee
- Saffy Swift
- Zane Zippy
- Imran Fast
- Stall Owner

- Runners
- Spectators

These are optional non-speaking parts.

A teacher could read the narrator's part if necessary. A teacher could also read the stage directions if the play is being used for group or guided reading.

Costume suggestions

Narrator
This child could either dress up in running clothes, or wear his or her usual school clothes.

Fun Run Organiser and Fun Run Helper
These children need sports clothes and flags or whistles. Stopwatches are also a good idea.

Martin Speed, Helen Health, Saffy Swift, Jimmy Quick, Zane Zippy, Imran Fast, optional runners and spectators
These children should all wear trainers and sports clothing.

Inky, Snake and Bee
These children should wear character masks. (See pages 94 to 96 for the mask templates.) They could also wear mouse, snake and bee costumes or, alternatively, running clothes. They should all wear trainers. Inky should have a magnifying glass.

Stall Owner
This child should wear an apron.

You will need...

A simple stage or stage area
For this play, a raised stage is not necessary; an area of free floor space will also work well.

Inky, Snake and Bee masks
Make up the character masks by using the templates provided, and following the instructions on page 78. Find pictures of the three characters, and get the children to colour in their own mask in the right colours.

A magnifying glass
If a real magnifying glass is not available, photocopy the picture provided on page 97. Glue the magnifying glass onto some thick card, colour it and cut it out.

The Golden Trainer trophy
Photocopy the picture provided on page 100. Glue the picture onto some thick card and cut it out. Glue the base of the trophy into a cardboard tube, and paint it gold.

A screen and toilets sign
Use a large folding screen to represent the toilets. (If a folding screen is not available, a curtain or a large free-standing board or easel would work well, too.) Write the word 'toilets' onto a thin piece of card and attach it to the screen.

A lemonade stall and bunting
Cover an up-turned cardboard box with a tablecloth and place some plastic cups, chocolate bars, fruit and other snacks on top. Add some bunting to the wall behind the stall.

Tree pictures
Paint several trees, and cut them out. (See page 75 for the 'Look at different types of tree activity'.)

Stage setting

Set the stage to look like a park. Fix some large tree pictures to the wall behind the stage. At the back of the stage on the right-hand side, set up a small stall selling drinks and chocolate and hang some bunting to the wall behind it. Place a large screen (representing the toilets) to the left-hand side of the stage. The narrator stands or sits beside this screen, to the left-hand side of the stage.

Song

Any children who were not given a speaking part can be encouraged to sing the song 'Run, Run, Run a Race' at the end of the play. Reproducible song lyrics are provided on page 54, and an audio track is available from the Jolly Learning website. Visit **jollylearning.co.uk/login**; log in or register; go to **My resources**; and enter the code: **JPLAYSBE1**.

Detective Inky in...
The Case of the Golden Trainer

> The narrator sits to the left-hand side of the stage.

Narrator: Today, Inky, Snake and Bee are doing a Fun Run in the park.

> Inky, Snake and Bee arrive on stage alongside lots of other fun runners all wearing trainers and dressed in sports kit or novelty costumes.

Inky, Snake and Bee: Hello!

Narrator: Inky, Snake and Bee are running with their friend, Martin Speed. Martin is very good at running.

> Martin does some star jumps in a display of his supreme fitness. All of the other runners gather around him.

Fun Run Organiser: Hello, everyone! Welcome to the Summer Fun Run!

Fun Run Helper: The first runner to cross the finish line wins the Golden Trainer.

> Fun Run Helper holds up the golden trainer.

All: Ooh! Aaah!

Fun Run Organiser: There are still ten minutes before the Fun Run starts, so if anyone needs to go to the toilet or get a drink, they can do that now.

Snake: I am going to get some lemonade. I am so thirsty. Ssss!

Inky: Ooh yes, me too!

Bee: And me!

> Inky, Snake and Bee cluster around the lemonade stall.

Martin Speed: I need to use the toilet. I will not be long.

> Helen, Jimmy, Saffy and Martin exit stage left. Everyone else exits stage right. The Fun Run Organiser and Helper take their flags and whistles and stand on the right-hand side of the stage, next to the stall. Martin stands, hidden by the screen, stage left.

Narrator: Soon, it is time for the Fun Run to start. All of the competitors line up. All, that is, except Martin, who is nowhere to be seen.

> All of the runners line up on stage, apart from Helen and Martin.

All: Where is Martin?

> Helen sneaks back onto the stage, after the other runners. All of the runners line up along the right-hand side of the stage in front of the Fun Run Organiser and Helper.

Helen Health: It's no use. We will have to start the Fun Run without him.

Inky: Hmmmmm.....

Fun Run Organiser: Ready... Steady... GO!

> The Fun Run Organiser and Helper blow their whistles or wave their flags to start the race. Inky, Snake, Bee, and all of the other runners run around the room, with Helen in the lead.

Saffy Swift: (Breathily) This hill is so steep!

Jimmy Quick: (Also breathily) Yes! I am all out of breath!

All runners: Puff... pant... puff...

Helen Health: I am winning!

> Helen crosses the finish line first. The Fun Run Organiser is just about to hand her the Golden Trainer when, suddenly, there is a shout from off stage.

Martin Speed: (Shouting) Help, help! Let me out!

Bee: That's Martin!

> The Fun Run Helper goes over to the screen at the left-hand side of the stage and pretends to open a door.

Fun Run Helper: He's in here!

> Martin comes out of the toilets.

Martin Speed: Someone locked me in the toilet so I couldn't run in the race!

All: (Stop and turn to the audience) Dun, dun, daaah!

Fun Run Helper: How awful!

Fun Run Organiser: Who would do that?

Inky: This is a case for Detective Inky! I will discover who locked you in, Martin.

> Inky whips out a large magnifying glass and holds it up.

Snake: Martin must have been locked in while we were having our drinks.

Zane Zippy: Yes, that must be what happened.

Inky: (To Jimmy) Where were you, Jimmy Quick, when we were having our drinks?

Jimmy Quick: I was by the swings, doing some stretches with Imran.

Imran Fast: Yes, he was.

Bee and Snake: We saw him there, too.

Inky: Hmmmm....

Inky: (To Saffy) Where were you, Saffy Swift, when we were having our drinks?

Saffy Swift: I was sitting under some trees in the shade.

Imran Fast: Yes, that's true. She was sitting under the trees.

All: (Loudly) Hmmmmm...

Inky: (To Helen) Where were you, Helen Health, when we were getting drinks?

Helen Health: I was... um... getting some chocolate at the stall.

Stall owner: I cannot remember seeing Helen...

	Helen fidgets on the spot.

Snake: (To Helen) Helen, why are you fidgeting so much?

	Helen stops fidgeting.

Helen Health: I am not fidgeting!

Inky: You were fidgeting, and now you have gone bright red! Helen, did you lock Martin in the toilet so that he couldn't run?

Helen Health: (Sheepishly) Yes, it was me. Martin is so quick that he always wins the Fun Run, and this time I wanted to win for once. I'm sorry.

Fun Run Organiser: Well, we cannot give you the prize now. If you had not stopped Martin running, he might have won.

Jimmy Quick: Martin should have the Golden Trainer to make up for being locked in the toilet.

	The Fun Run Organiser gives Martin the Golden Trainer, and he holds it up.

All: Hip, hip, hooray!

THE END

Tips for performing
- Speak slowly and clearly.
- Do not worry if you forget a line or make a mistake.
- Enjoy it!

Detective Inky in...
The Case of the Vanishing Cakes

This play has eight speaking parts. If you are using this play for group or guided reading, simply allocate the parts and provide one copy of the play for each child. (See pages 28 to 31 for a reproducible play script.) If you are intending to perform the play, the following pages provide suggested costumes for each character and outline the props necessary for performing the play.

Characters

- Narrator
- Inky
- Bee
- Town Mayor

- Eddy Bread
- Sammy Biscuits
- Laila Lemons

- Snake

- Cooks
- Helpers
These are optional non-speaking parts.

A teacher could read the narrator's part if necessary. A teacher could also read the stage directions if the play is being used for group or guided reading.

Costume suggestions

Narrator
This child could either dress up in an apron, like the cooks, or wear his or her usual school clothes.

Inky, Snake and Bee
These children should wear character masks. (See pages 94 to 96 for the mask templates.) Bee should also wear an apron, and Inky should have a magnifying glass.

Town Mayor
This child will need a Mayor's costume, including a chain, robes and a hat if possible. (See page 101 for a chain template.)

Eddy Bread, Sammy Biscuits, Laila Lemons, optional cooks and helpers
These children will need to wear aprons or chefs' hats.

You will need...

A simple stage or stage area
For this play, a raised stage is not necessary; an area of free floor space will also work well.

Inky, Snake and Bee masks
Make up the character masks by using the templates provided, and following the instructions on page 78. Find pictures of the three characters, and get the children to colour in their own mask in the right colours.

A magnifying glass
If a real magnifying glass is not available, photocopy the picture provided on page 97. Glue the magnifying glass onto some thin card, colour and cut out.

Baking paraphernalia
All of the cooks will need aprons or chefs' hats. Bowls, wooden spoons and baking ingredients will also be useful.

A toy kitchen and oven
If a toy kitchen is not available, cardboard boxes could be painted to look like kitchen worktops. A larger box, with opening flaps, could be painted to look like an oven.

Flower pots and chairs
If real or false plants are not available, make some potted plants using the templates on pages 102 to 103. These will be arranged with some school chairs to form a garden.

Stage setting

Set the stage to look like a Town Hall. Set up some toy kitchen sets (or painted cardboard boxes) on the left-hand side of the stage to form the Town Hall's kitchen. Make a small garden area dotted with pot plants and chairs on the right-hand side of the stage. The narrator stands or sits to the left-hand side of the stage.

Song

Any children who were not given a speaking part can be encouraged to sing the song 'All the Lovely Cakes' at the end of the play. Reproducible song lyrics are provided on page 55, and an audio track is available from the Jolly Learning website. Visit **jollylearning.co.uk/login**; log in or register; go to **My resources**; and enter the code: **JPLAYSBE1**.

Detective Inky in... The Case of the Vanishing Cakes

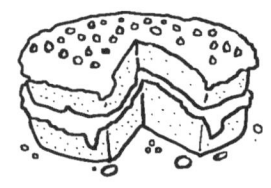

 The narrator sits to the left-hand side of the stage. Bee and the other cooks are in the kitchen with the Mayor. Snake, Inky and the helpers are in the garden.

Narrator: This weekend, there is a Cake Contest at the Town Hall. Bee is going to take part. Inky and Snake have come along to support her.

Snake: And to eat all of the yummy cakes!

Narrator: Bee and all of the other cooks gather in the kitchen, and the Mayor explains the rules.

Mayor: All of the cooks have just one hour to bake their cakes. Then we will try all of the cakes, and the baker of the best cake wins a prize.

 The cooks all go and stand by their bowls.

Mayor: Okay, you can start cooking!

 All of the cooks frantically unpack their flour and eggs, and start mixing. The Mayor walks around, talking to each cook in turn.

Mayor: So, Eddy Bread, what are you going to make for us today?

Eddy Bread: I am going to make marvellous, super-duper, scrummy chocolate cupcakes.

Mayor: Mmmmm, that sounds wonderful.

Bee: Buzz buzz... Where is my butter? I know I had it somewhere...

Mayor: And you, Sammy Biscuits, are you going to make jammy biscuits for us?

Sammy Biscuits: Er, no, I am going to make blueberry muffins.

Mayor: Mmmm, yes, blueberry muffins are definitely the best sort of muffin.

Laila Lemons: I am going to make a lovely lemon drizzle cake, with lots of lemon zest in it.

Mayor: (Quietly, to the audience) Yuck! I hate lemons. Pah!

> The Mayor turns to Bee.

Mayor: What are you cooking for us, Bee?

Bee: I am going to make an apple and raisin cake, with chopped hazelnuts.

Mayor: Yummy, yummy! That sounds good.

Narrator: Soon it was time for all of the cakes to go in the oven.

Bee: I am so pleased with my cake!

Eddy, Laila, Sammy and the other cooks: Ooh yes, me too!

Mayor: Well, we have some time before the cakes will be ready. We should sit in the garden for a while.

Narrator: Everyone goes out into the garden except the Mayor, who slips away quietly. Inky and Snake are waiting in the garden for Bee.

Inky: How is the Cake Contest going, Bee?

Bee: Everything has gone quite well so far, I think.

Snake: I bet your cake looked splendid, Bee.

Bee: Ooh, I hope so, but everyone's cakes looked good.

Eddy Bread: All of our cakes will be baked now. We should go and take them out before they burn.

All cooks: Yes, let's go in.

> The cooks hurry off into the kitchen and open the oven.

Eddy Bread: My cakes! My marvellous, super-duper, scrummy chocolate cupcakes, they have gone!

Sammy Biscuits: All of our cakes have vanished!

Bee: Sniff, sniff.

Inky: What's that? All of the cakes have vanished? This is a case for detective Inky!

> Inky whips out her huge magnifying glass.

Inky: I will follow all of the clues in the hunt for the missing cakes!

Laila Lemons: Not all of the cakes have gone. My lemon drizzle cake is still here.

> Laila holds up her cake.

Snake: That's odd!

Inky: Yes, it is very odd.

Bee: Look here. There is a trail of chocolate chips and raisins.

> Inky, Snake and all of the cooks follow the trail across the stage to find…

Inky: Mayor! What are you doing here? You are covered in crumbs!

Sammy Biscuits: Did you eat all of our cakes?

Mayor: (With a mouth full of cake) Cakes? No, I didn't touch the cakes.

Laila Lemons: That's funny. I heard you say that you didn't like lemons, and now all of the cakes have vanished apart from my lemon drizzle cake.

All: Yes!

Inky: And you have chocolate all around your mouth!

Mayor: Oh, it's true. I ate the cakes. I just cannot resist the smell of hot cakes.

Inky: We all like cake, but eating all of the cakes was very greedy and selfish of you, Mayor.

Mayor: Sniff, sniff, yes, I am sorry. I was very selfish indeed.

Eddy Bread: As a punishment for eating all of the cakes, you should clean the kitchen for us!

All cooks: Yes, what a good punishment.

Mayor: But... But it's a dreadful, dirty mess!

Inky: Go and clean the kitchen, Mayor. And while you are doing that, we will all have some of this lovely lemon drizzle cake!

> The Mayor goes off to clean the kitchen, and everyone else sits down to enjoy the lemon drizzle cake.

Mayor: I'm feeling a little sick now...

THE END

Tips for performing
- Speak slowly and clearly.
- Do not worry if you forget a line or make a mistake.
- Enjoy it!

Part 4: Discoveries plays

The Un-Lucky Ring

This play has ten speaking parts. If you are using this play for group or guided reading, simply allocate the parts and provide one copy of the play for each child. (See pages 34 to 37 for a reproducible play script.) If you are intending to perform the play, the following pages provide suggested costumes for each character and outline the props necessary for performing the play.

Characters

- Narrator 1
- Tom
- Megan
- Mum
- Miss Patel

- Narrator 2
- Mr Evans
- Dad

- Bobby
- Jasmin

- Other children in the class
These are optional non-speaking parts.

A teacher could read the narrators' parts if necessary. A teacher could also read the stage directions if the play is being used for group or guided reading.

Costume suggestions

Narrator 1 and Narrator 2
These children should wear their usual school clothes.

Tom and Megan
These children should wear the clothes that they usually wear to school. At the beginning of the play, they should also wear an additional sweatshirt (not school uniform), which they can take off during the play. They will also need Wellington boots and umbrellas.

Miss Patel and Mr Evans
These children should dress like their teachers. They will also need paper and pencils to hand out during the play.

Mum and Dad
These children should dress like their own parents. They will also need Wellington boots and umbrellas.

Bobby, Jasmin and other children without speaking parts
These children should wear the clothes that they usually wear to school.

You will need...

A simple stage or stage area
For this play, a raised stage is not necessary; an area of free floor space will also work well.

A gold ring
Use a large gold-coloured toy ring for this. Alternatively, make a ring by following the instructions on page 104.

A desk or small table, and two (or more) chairs
Use a school desk and chairs for this.

Tree pictures
See page 75 for the 'Look at different types of tree activity'. Research the different kinds of tree that grow locally. Look at pictures of trees in books, or take the children for a walk around the school grounds or the local park, and point out the various different types of tree. Provide a large sheet of paper for each child in the class. The children each paint a picture of a different type of tree. The best of these pictures can then be stuck to the wall behind the stage so as to form a small forest.

Umbrellas, paper, pencils and a bell
The umbrellas are needed for the beginning of the play by Mum, Dad, Tom and Megan. The children playing the teachers bring on the paper and pencils later on in the play. The bell is not used on stage; a child or a teacher should ring it off stage at the right moment in the play.

Stage setting

Set the left-hand side of the stage to look like a study or a classroom, with a desk and two chairs. Both chairs should face the audience. In front of the desk, place four umbrellas and four pairs of Wellington boots in a line. On the right-hand side of the stage, fix some tree pictures to the wall to form a little forest. Near the back of the stage under one of the tree pictures, place the gold ring.

Song

Any children who were not given a speaking part can be encouraged to sing the song 'Lucky Ring' at the end of the play. Reproducible song lyrics are provided on page 56, and an audio track is available from the Jolly Learning website. Visit **jollylearning.co.uk/login**; log in or register; go to **My resources**; and enter the code: **JPLAYSBE1**.

The Un-Lucky Ring

> Tom and Megan are sitting at the desk in their non-school outfits. Megan is studying hard. Tom is sitting with his head on the desk and is snoring loudly.

Narrator 1: Megan has been studying hard all day because she has an important maths test tomorrow.

Narrator 2: Tom also has a test on Monday. His is a spelling test, but he has not been studying quite as hard as Megan.

Megan: Two times two is four; two times three is six; two times four is eight...

> Tom sits with his head on the desk and snores loudly.

Dad: Megan, you've been studying for hours now. You should have a rest. Why not come for a walk in the woods with me?

Tom: (Wakes up with a start) What's that? A walk? What a good plan! I'll go and get Mum.

> Tom exits stage left and comes back on stage with Mum.

Mum: (To Megan) Have you finished all of your maths practice now, Megan?

Megan: Yes, I think so.

Dad: She has been studying all day.

Mum: (To Tom) Have you learnt all of your spellings, Tom?

Tom: Ummm, yes... I think so.

Mum: Come on then you two; let's put on our boots and go for a walk.

> Mum, Dad, Tom and Megan all put on their boots and pick up their umbrellas. They go across to the right-hand side of the stage and walk around by the tree pictures.

Mum: What a lovely walk! It's so nice to be out in the fresh air.

Tom: (Bending down to pick up the gold ring) Look what I've found!

Dad: What is it, Tom?

Tom: It's a gold ring, with an owl on it.

> Mum, Dad and Megan all cluster around Tom.

Mum: The owl is made from gemstones. How lucky!

Tom: Lucky? Hmmmm...

> Dad stretches out his hand and looks up at the sky.

Dad: Oh no, it's raining. Come on; let's go home.

> All put up their umbrellas and walk off stage right. Tom and Megan take off their non-school sweatshirts so that they are ready for school.

Narrator 1: Now it is Monday, the day of Megan's maths test and Tom's spelling test.

> Megan and Tom come back on stage right and walk around by the tree pictures.

Narrator 2: Tom and Megan are walking to school.

Megan: Did you learn all of your spellings Tom?

Tom: No, but I'm not bothered. My test is not until this afternoon, and my owl ring will bring me good luck anyway.

Megan: My test is this morning and I am so nervous.

Tom: Why not take my lucky owl ring to your test? You can give it back to me at lunch time.

> Tom gives Megan the ring. They arrive at Megan's classroom, and Megan sits down at the desk.

Megan: Thanks, Tom! I'll see you later.

Tom: Bye!

> Tom walks off stage right. Bobby comes on stage left and sits down next to Megan. If possible, other children walk on stage, too, bringing their chairs with them. These children sit down next to Megan and Bobby. Miss Patel walks on stage.

Miss Patel: Good morning, children.

Bobby, Megan and other children: Good morning, Miss Patel.

Miss Patel: I hope you have all practised your maths over the weekend.

> Miss Patel hands out paper and pencils to the children.

Miss Patel: Write your name at the top and your answers underneath. Are you all ready? What is two times eleven?

Narrator 1: Megan and her friends complete the test, and Miss Patel collects up their answers.

> Miss Patel collects up the papers and looks at Megan's test.

Miss Patel: (To Megan) My goodness, Megan, you've got them all right! That is excellent!

> The bell rings off stage. All of the children stand up to leave. Miss Patel and all of the children apart from Megan exit stage left. Megan walks over to the right-hand side of the stage and Tom walks on stage right.

Megan: Tom, your ring really is lucky! I got ten out of ten in my maths test! Here, take it back for your spelling test.

> Megan gives the ring back to Tom.

Megan: It will definitely bring you good luck for this afternoon.

> The bell rings again and Megan walks off stage right. Tom sits down at the desk. Jasmin comes on stage left and sits down next to Tom. If possible, other children walk on stage, too, bringing their chairs with them. These children sit down next to Tom and Jasmin. Mr Evans comes on stage and hands out paper and pencils.

Mr Evans: Good afternoon, children.

Jasmin and Tom (and other children): Good afternoon, Mr Evans.

Mr Evans: Now children, it's time for our spelling test. How do you spell 'because'?

Narrator 1: Tom clutches his owl ring tightly in the hope that it will bring him luck, but the spelling test is very hard...

Tom: Because... because... /b/, /i/, /k/, /o/, /zzz/ - bikoz!

Narrator 2: Soon the test is over, and Mr Evans collects the papers.

Mr Evans: Hand your answers to me, everyone.

🎭 All of the children hand their papers to Mr Evans, who looks at them one-by-one.

Mr Evans: (To Jasmin) Good, Jasmin, very good.
(To Tom) Tom! Not one of these is spelt correctly!

Tom: It's not my fault! My lucky ring must have run out of luck!

Mr Evans: Lucky ring? What lucky ring? Did you learn any of these spellings?

Tom: Um... Well, no, not really.

Mr Evans: You have to practise your spellings, Tom. You cannot just rely on luck.

🎭 Mr Evans and all of the children except Tom exit stage left. Megan walks on stage.

Megan: (To Tom) So, how was your spelling test?

Tom: I got every spelling wrong. My lucky ring was not so lucky after all!

THE END

Tips for performing
- Speak slowly and clearly.
- Do not worry if you forget a line or make a mistake.
- Enjoy it!

The Rainbow

This play has ten speaking parts. If you are using this play for group or guided reading, simply allocate the parts and provide one copy of the play for each child. (See pages 40 to 43 for a reproducible play script.) If you are intending to perform the play, the following pages provide suggested costumes for each character and outline the props necessary for performing the play.

Characters

- Narrator 1
- Narrator 2
- Sun

- Rain
- Snow
- Wind

- Two summer children
- Two winter children

- Rainbow
- Trees
- Flowers

These are non-speaking parts.

A teacher could read the narrators' parts if necessary. A teacher could also read the stage directions if the play is being used for group or guided reading.

Costume suggestions

Narrator 1 and Narrator 2
These children should wear their usual school clothes.

Sun, Rain, Snow, Wind and Rainbow
These children should wear the weather sandwich boards; see pages 78 for instructions and pages 106 to 112 for templates. In addition, Sun should wear yellow clothes; Snow should wear white clothes; Wind should wear white or blue clothes; Rainbow should wear multi-coloured clothes (where possible); and Rain should wear grey clothes and Wellington boots. The child playing the rain could also use a watering can to mime raining.

Trees and Flowers
These children should both wear green or brown clothes. In addition, the Trees should hold branches and the Flowers should hold flowers; see page 105 for instructions and templates.

Summer and winter children
The two summer children should wear light summer clothes and flip-flops. The two winter children should wear warm winter clothes, woolly hats, scarves and Wellington boots; these children will also need an umbrella each.

You will need...

A raised stage platform
This play works best with a raised stage platform that allows the children playing the weather characters to be above the other performers.

Weather sandwich boards
Make the sandwich boards for Sun, Rain, Snow, Wind and Rainbow according to the instructions on page 78 using the templates on pages 106 to 112.

Tree branches and flowers
Photocopy the leaves and flowers on page 105; stick onto card, colour, cut out and attach to green or brown pipe cleaners.

A bucket of snowballs, a watering can and umbrellas
Scrunch up some white scrap paper or tissue paper to make snowballs. Put the snowballs into a bag or bucket for the child playing Snow. The child playing Rain can use a watering can, and the two winter children will need an umbrella each.

Cloud pictures
Draw some large clouds shapes on white paper, or use the templates on pages 107 and 112. Cut them out and stick them to the wall behind the stage.

A kite
The summer children will need a kite. If a toy kite is not available, make a kite by following the instructions on page 104.

Stage setting

Set the stage very simply, with large clouds fixed to the wall behind a raised platform. The narrators sit cross-legged at the front of the stage, towards the left-hand side. The Trees and Flowers children stand in front of the stage towards the right-hand side.

Song

Any children who were not given a speaking part can be encouraged to sing 'The Rainbow Song' at the end of the play. Reproducible song lyrics are provided on page 57, and an audio track is available from the Jolly Learning website. Visit **jollylearning.co.uk/login**; log in or register; go to **My resources**; and enter the code: **JPLAYSBE1**.

The Rainbow

> The narrators sit to the left-hand side of the stage.

Narrator 1: There are lots of different sorts of weather.

Narrator 2: It can be rainy...

> Rain walks on stage right, stands next to the narrators and mimes raining with his or her fingers, or with the can.

Narrator 1: Or it can be snowy...

> Snow walks on stage right, stands next to Rain and gently drops tissue paper snowballs from his or her bucket onto the stage.

Narrator 2: Or it can be sunny...

> Sun walks on stage right, stands next to Snow and stretches out his or her arms like the rays of the sun.

Narrator 1: Or it can be windy...

> Wind walks on stage right, stands next to Sun, and blows onto his or her hands, with cheeks puffed out.

Narrator 2: Or, there can be a rainbow!

> Rainbow does not walk on stage.

Narrator 2: (Shouting) Rainbow! RAIN-BOW!
(To Narrator 1) Where is the rainbow?

Narrator 1: I think the rainbow is a bit shy. We might have to wait until it is ready to come out.

Narrator 2: Depending on the season, a different sort of weather takes its turn in the sky.

> Snow, Sun and Wind exit stage right. Snow picks up the snowballs and puts them back in the bucket. Rain walks into the middle of the stage. Trees and Flowers stand in front of the stage on the right-hand side, holding out their leaves and flowers.

Rain: I am the rain, and I like to make lots of big puddles for children to splash about in.

 Rain pretends to rain all over the front of the stage. Trees and Flowers raise their arms and hold up their leaves and flowers. The two winter children walk in front of the stage from stage left wearing boots and holding umbrellas. They pretend to splash about in puddles.

Narrator 1: Without the rain, all of the trees and flowers would die and there would be no food crops to eat.

 Rain exits stage right and the winter children exit to left. Sun enters stage right and stands in the middle of the stage.

Sun: I am the sun and I make lots of lovely sunshine, which heats up the ground.

 Sun raises his or her arms, like the sun's rays, and two summer children walk in front of the stage from the left wearing flip flops. They skip about in the sunshine.

Narrator 2: The sun also makes food for all of the trees and flowers, which helps them to grow big and tall.

 Trees and Flowers stretch out their arms as the narrator explains this. Then, Sun exits stage right and the summer children exit to the left. Snow enters stage right and stands in the middle of the stage, holding the bucket of tissue paper snowballs.

Snow: I am the snow, and I fall instead of rain when it is very cold.

 Two winter children walk in front of the stage from the left wearing hats and scarves, and Snow gently throws paper snowballs at them. The children pick up the snowballs and throw them at each other. Trees and Flowers shiver with cold.

Narrator 1: You often see snow on the tops of mountains. When it snows, children like to have snowball fights and make snowmen.

Children: We love the snow!

 Snow exits stage right and the winter children exit to the left with the snowballs. Wind enters stage right and stands in the middle of the stage. Two summer children walk in front of the stage from the left carrying a kite.

Wind: I am the wind and I like to blow everything about. When it is windy, children like to fly kites.

> One of the summer children takes the end of the kite's string and the other takes the kite and lifts it up into the air. Trees and Flowers bend and sway in the wind.

Narrator 2: As well as blowing kites about, the wind also blows the seeds from trees and flowers onto fresh soil so that they can grow into new trees and flowers.

> Trees and Flowers continue to sway in the wind as the narrator explains this.

Narrator 1: All of the different sorts of weather are important.

> Wind exits stage right and the summer children exit to the left.

Narrator 2: Normally, the different sorts of weather take turns in the sky, but today the rain and the sun are having a disagreement.

> Rain and Sun enter stage right and stand in the middle of the stage.

Rain: It should be my turn in the sky today. Look at those flowers! They are wilting and they need a drink.

> Flowers and Trees flop over and let their leaves and flowers droop by dangling them on the floor.

Sun: No, it should be my turn in the sky. It has been cloudy all week and the trees have had no sunlight. They need sunlight otherwise they cannot grow.

Rain: But it's my turn!

Sun: No, it's my turn!

Rain: It's my turn!

Sun: It's my turn!

Rain: It's my turn!

Sun: It's my turn!

Narrator 1: The rain and the sun argued for a long time.

> Snow and Wind enter stage right and stand next to Sun and Rain.

Narrator 2: The wind and the snow grew tired of listening to them argue.

Snow: We are fed up with listening to you argue.

Wind: If you cannot agree about who should be in the sky today, why not go out in the sky together?

Rain: That sounds like a good plan to me. What do you think, Sun?

Sun: Yes, I think we should share the sky. After all, the trees and flowers need sun and rain to live.

Narrator 1: So the rain and the sun went out in the sky at the same time.

Narrator 2: The rain fell in big droplets, and the sun shone brightly.

> Rain mimes raining and Sun stretches out his or her arms like rays.

Narrator 1: The trees and flowers stopped wilting and started growing again.

> Trees and Flowers stop drooping and stretch up, holding out their leaves and flowers.

Narrator 2: And then, suddenly, something wonderful happened: as the sunlight shone in the raindrops, it made big colourful stripes in the sky.

> Rainbow enters stage right and stands in between Rain and Sun. The summer and winter children enter from the left and point at the rainbow.

Children: Look, it's a rainbow!

Rain: (To Sun) Look what we have made!

Sun: It's lovely!

Wind: And you could not have made it by yourselves.

Snow: You could only have made it together.

Narrator 1: And from that point on, the rain and the sun never argued again.

THE END

Tips for performing
- Speak slowly and clearly.
- Do not worry if you forget a line or make a mistake.
- Enjoy it!

Part 5: Using the plays

Comprehension and discussion questions
Pages 46 to 51

Once the children have read a play, it is important to talk about it with them and ensure that they have understood it and remembered what they have read. For each play, there are two sets of questions: **comprehension questions** and **discussion questions**. Read both sets of questions to the children and encourage them to discuss their answers as a group.

1. The **comprehension questions** simply require the children to recall what happened in the play. Ask the children these questions as soon as they have read the play.

2. The **discussion questions** require the children to think more deeply about what they have read. Often, there is no single correct answer to these questions. Instead, the questions are intended to develop the children's reasoning and communication skills. What matters is not so much *what* the children think, but *how* they think and how they communicate their thoughts. When you ask a question, do not ask the children to put their hands up and answer immediately; instead, encourage them to discuss it in pairs or small groups before answering. You could then nominate a child from each group to answer for their whole group. This approach encourages the children to communicate well with each other.

The plays also highlight a number of **core values**: for example, the importance of sharing. Teachers can use these plays to prompt discussions about the following values:

1. **Sharing** (highlighted in *How the Zebras Got Their Stripes, Why Anansi the Spider has Eight Thin Legs, The Case of the Vanishing Cakes, The Un-Lucky Ring* and *The Rainbow*),
2. **Playing fairly** (highlighted in *The Case of the Golden Trainer*),
3. **Working hard** (highlighted in *The Un-Lucky Ring*),
4. **Working together** (highlighted in *How the Zebras Got Their Stripes* and *The Rainbow*),
5. **Being kind to others** (highlighted in *How the Zebras Got Their Stripes, The Case of the Vanishing Cakes* and *The Case of the Golden Trainer*).

Songs
Pages 52 to 57

There is a song for each play. These can be used whether the children are performing the plays or just reading them. Songs are particularly helpful for children who have English as a second language, because the rhythm and melody help to make the words more memorable. The songs also help those children who were not given a speaking part to feel included in the play. Reproducible song lyrics are provided on pages 52 to 57, and an audio track of each song is available from the Jolly Learning website. Visit **jollylearning.co.uk/login**; log in or register; go to **My resources**; and enter the code: **JPLAYSBE1**.

Reading comprehension and writing activities

After a child has read a story or a play, it is important to find out how much of it he or she has understood and to fill in any gaps in his or her vocabulary knowledge or understanding. Pages 58 to 71 provide a number of activities that can be used to improve vocabulary and reading comprehension.

Story sequencing Pages 58 to 63

One simple way to assess reading comprehension after reading a play is to use the story sequencing strips on pages 58 to 63. Divide the children into pairs or small groups and provide one set of story sequencing strips for each pair or group of children. (Make sure that the strips are cut up and shuffled beforehand, because they are in the correct order on the page.) Encourage the children to work together to put the strips in the right order.

Retelling the story Pages 64 to 65

Another simple way to find out whether the children have understood a play is to ask them to retell the story in their own words. Depending on the ability and age of the children, you might like to ask them to rewrite the play as a story in their own words, retell the story orally in pairs or small groups, or use the comic strip template on page 64 to create a comic strip version of the play. If your class is using the comic strip template, encourage the children to write the title of the play at the top of the page, and then draw what happens in the play in the boxes underneath, numbering the boxes as they draw in them. More able children can use the template on page 65, and write what happens in the spaces underneath each picture. Some children will need more than one copy of the comic strip template.

Looking at the characters Pages 66 to 71

After reading or performing a play with the children, discuss the characteristics of the main characters. What do they look like? Are they kind or unkind? What other adjectives could you use to describe them? Would you like to be friends with them or not? Why (not)? Encourage the children to look through the plays and spot any words used to describe the main characters. For example, in *How the Zebras Got Their Stripes,* the baboon is described as 'selfish' and 'grumpy'; the gazelle is 'hot'; the antelope is 'thirsty'; and the cheetah is 'brave'. In *Why Anansi the Spider has Eight Thin Legs,* Anansi says he is 'hungry' and he is described as 'greedy' by Crow; in *The Case of the Vanishing Cakes,* the mayor is described as 'selfish'; and in *The Case of the Golden Trainer,* Martin Speed is described as 'quick'. Use the activities on pages 66 to 71 to help the children begin to look at character. Make sure that they understand the meanings of all of the words used on the worksheet before asking them to complete it.

How the Zebras Got Their Stripes

Comprehension questions

1. What colour were the Zebras at the beginning of the play?

2. How did the Zebras get their stripes in the play?

3. What did the Baboon want to keep for himself?

4. Which characters does the Baboon frighten away?

5. What happened to the Baboon at the end of the play?

Discussion questions

1. In the play, the Zebras got their stripes when they were scorched by the campfire. Do you think this is really how zebras get their stripes? Why (not)?

2. Do you think the Baboon was selfish when he kept the river all to himself? Have you ever been selfish: for example, with your toys or sweets? Have you ever tried to stop someone joining in with a game? What happens when someone is selfish?

3. Do you think the Baboon deserved to lose all of the fur on his bottom?

Core values

1. **Sharing:** why is it important that all of the animals share the river?

2. **Working together:** the Zebras all work together to show the Baboon that he needs to share the river. Why is it important to work together?

3. **Being kind to others:** was the Baboon kind to the other animals? Should he have been? Why (not)?

 # Why Anansi the Spider has Eight Thin Legs

Comprehension questions

1. At the beginning of the play, were Anansi's legs long or short?

2. What happens to Anansi's legs at the end of the play?

3. How many legs does Anansi have?

4. What are all of Anansi's friends doing when he meets them?

5. What does Anansi tie to every cooking pot, bowl and wok?

Discussion questions

1. Do you think Anansi was greedy? Have you ever been a bit greedy? What happens when someone is greedy?

2. In the play, Anansi got his long, thin legs when everyone pulled on strands of web that were tied to his legs. Do you think this is really how spiders get their long, thin legs?

3. Why do you think spiders' legs are long and thin? Do some research to find out if you are right.

Core values

1. **Sharing:** all of Anansi's friends share their food with him. What happens when we share things with other people? Is it important to share? Why (not)?

Detective Inky in... The Case of the Golden Trainer

Comprehension questions

1. What were the runners trying to win?

2. What happened to stop Martin running in the race?

3. In the race, who crossed the finish line first?

4. Why did Helen lock Martin in the toilet?

5. Who was given the trophy at the end of the play?

Discussion questions

1. Did Helen deserve to have the trophy? Why (not)?

2. Why did Helen go red when Inky and Snake found out that she had locked Martin in the toilet? What is it called when we go red? (Explain that some of us blush when we are embarrassed or when we feel guilty.)

3. Do you think Helen cheated in the race when she stopped Martin taking part? Have you ever cheated: for example, in a game or a race? What happens when people cheat?

Core values

1. **Playing fairly:** why is it important that we play fairly in games and races? If someone cheats in a race, can they really say they have won it?

2. **Being kind to others:** do you think Helen was kind to Martin? What could she have done instead?

Detective Inky in... The Case of the Vanishing Cakes

Comprehension questions

1. What were all of the cooks making in the play?

2. What happened to the missing cakes?

3. Which cake was not stolen?

4. What do Inky, Snake, Bee and the cooks follow to find the Mayor?

5. What was the Mayor's punishment?

Discussion questions

1. Remind the children that the Mayor in this play was quite selfish and greedy when he stole the cakes and ate them. Which characters in the other plays we have read were selfish or greedy? (Depending on which plays the children have read, remind them about the following characters: Anansi the spider, who was quite greedy because he wanted to eat some of everyone's lunch; the Baboon, who was selfish and greedy when he kept the river to himself; and Helen who was selfish because she wanted to win the race so much that she stopped Martin competing in it.)

2. As a punishment for eating all of the cakes, the mayor has to clean the dirty, messy kitchen. Do you think he deserved this punishment? Why (not)?

3. Do you think the mayor was a good judge for a baking competition? How could he have been better?

Core values

1. **Sharing:** at the end of the play, all of the cooks except the Mayor share Laila's lemon drizzle cake. Why is it good to share things with other people? Have you ever shared something with other people?

2. **Being kind to others:** do you think the mayor was kind to the cooks? How could he have behaved instead?

The Un-Lucky Ring

Comprehension questions

1. What does Tom find in the woods?

2. What test does Megan have on Monday?

3. What test does Tom have on Monday?

4. How does Megan do in her maths test?

5. How does Tom do in his spelling test?

Discussion questions

1. In the play, why does Tom think his ring is lucky? (Mum tells Tom that he was lucky to find the ring, and Megan tells Tom that the ring helped her to get ten out ten in her maths test.)

2. Do you think the ring was lucky? Do you believe in luck? Do you have a lucky object? Why do you think some people might believe in luck?

3. Why do you think Megan got full marks in her maths test? Why did Tom get none of his spellings right?

4. What would you do if you found a ring in the forest?

Core values

1. **Sharing:** remind the children that Tom lent his ring Megan to bring her luck in her maths test. Ask the children if they have ever lent any of their possessions to someone else.

2. **Working hard:** why is it important that we work hard and do our best?

The Rainbow

Comprehension questions

1. Do the trees and flowers need the rain? Why?

2. Do the trees and flowers need the sun? Why?

3. What do the children do when it is windy?

4. What do the children do when it snows?

5. Does it snow when it is hot or when it is cold?

Discussion questions

1. In the play, the Rain and the Sun argue about whose turn it is to be in the sky. Do you ever argue with your friends or your brothers and sisters? How can you end an argument?

2. We have different kinds of weather in different seasons. Which is your favourite season? Why?

3. In the play, the Rainbow was made when the sunlight shone through the raindrops. Do you think this is really how rainbows are made? Look in books or use the internet to find out if you are right.

Core values

1. **Sharing:** remind the children that the different sorts of weather take turns to be in the sky. Ask the children if they ever take turns: for example, in a game or with toys. Why is it important that we share and take turns?

2. **Working together:** remind the children that a Rainbow is made when the Rain and the Sun work together. Neither the Rain nor the Sun could have made the Rainbow by themselves. The Rain and the Sun also work together to keep the trees and flowers alive. Have you ever made something by working together with someone else that you could not have made by yourself?

Song for *How the Zebras Got Their Stripes*
Sing to the tune of 'The Wheels on the Bus'.

The Mean Baboon

Gazelle and Antelope tried to get a drink,
And have a little swim,
On a hot day.
Baboon said, "No!" and frightened them away.
He frightened them away.

Cheetah came along and asked for a drink.
"Just a little drink,
On a hot day."
Baboon said, "No!" and frightened her away.
He frightened her away.

The Zebras came along and told Baboon,
"You must share!
You mustn't be mean!"
Baboon said, "No!" but the Zebras stood firm.
"DO AS YOU'RE TOLD!"

Baboon got cross and ran at the Zebras,
They all got scorched,
By the campfire.
The Zebras got stripes and Baboon lost fur,
From his big red bottom!

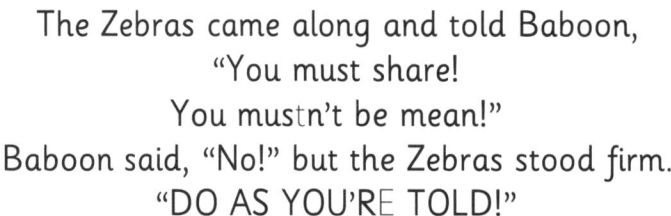

52

🎵 **Song** for *Why Anansi the Spider has Eight Thin Legs* 🎵
Sing to the tune of 'Alice the Camel'.

Anansi the Spider Likes...

Anansi the spider likes carrots,
Anansi the spider likes carrots,
Anansi the spider likes carrots,
So go, Anansi, go!
Boom, boom, boom...

Anansi the spider likes melon,
Anansi the spider likes melon,
Anansi the spider likes melon,
So go, Anansi, go!
Boom, boom, boom...

Anansi the spider likes salad,
Anansi the spider likes salad,
Anansi the spider likes salad,
So go, Anansi, go!
Boom, boom, boom...

Anansi the spider likes stir-fry,
Anansi the spider likes stir-fry,
Anansi the spider likes stir-fry,
So go, Anansi, go!
Boom, boom, boom...

Anansi the spider likes sandwiches,
Anansi the spider likes sandwiches,
Anansi the spider likes sandwiches,
Anansi likes his food!

Song for *The Case of the Golden Trainer*
Sing to the tune of 'Row, Row, Row Your Boat'.

Run, Run, Run a Race

Run, run, run a race,
Chatting as we go,
Zipping, zooming, sprinting, bolting,
We are never slow!

Run, run, run a race,
Once around the swings,
Bouncing, bounding, leaping, jumping,
Run like you're on springs!

Run, run, run a race,
Twice around the track,
Tramping, trotting, shuffling, plodding,
We are at the back!

Run, run, run a race,
Up and down the hill,
Wheezing, grunting, puffing, panting,
Right up to the mill!

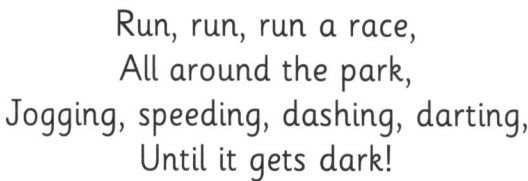

Run, run, run a race,
All around the park,
Jogging, speeding, dashing, darting,
Until it gets dark!

Song for *The Case of the Vanishing Cakes*
Sing to the tune of 'He's Got the Whole World in his Hands'.

All the Lovely Cakes

I love blueberry muffins,
Yum, yum, yum!
I like apple and raisins,
In my tum!
I eat chocolate cupcakes,
One by one!
I scoff the whole lot in one go!
(chomping noises)

I love big plum cakes,
Yum, yum, yum!
I like cherry and peaches,
In my tum!
I eat sweet teacakes,
One by one!
I scoff the whole lot in one go!
(chomping noises)

I love rich fudge cake,
Yum, yum, yum!
I like roasted fig cake,
In my tum!
I eat strawberry shortcakes,
One by one!
I scoff the whole lot in one go!
(chomping noises)

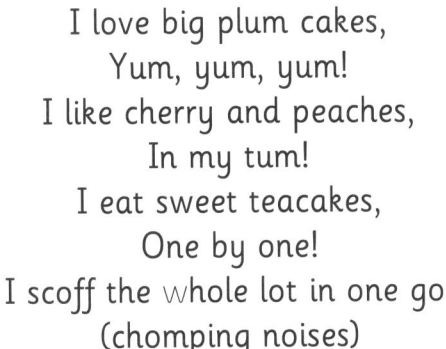
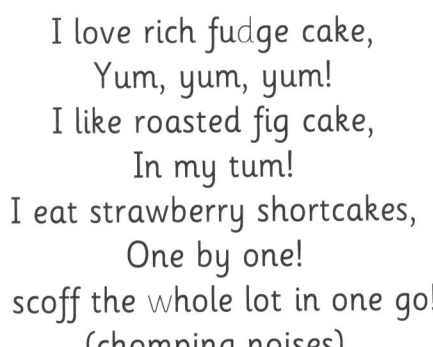
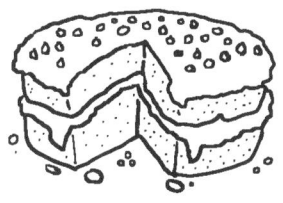

Song for *The Un-Lucky Ring*
Sing to the tune of 'Heads, Shoulders, Knees and Toes'.

Lucky Ring

This is my lucky ring,
Lucky ring!
It brings me lots of luck,
Lots of luck,
For maths and spelling tests at school!
This is my lucky ring,
Lucky ring!

I found it in the woods,
In the woods.
While on a rainy walk,
Rainy walk,
I saw a glint, and bent to see,
A lucky ring for me,
Ring for me!

On it is a golden owl,
Golden owl.
The eyes are made from gems,
Made from gems.
It shines and glistens in the light!
This is my lucky ring,
Lucky ring!

Song for *The Rainbow*
Sing to the tune of 'If You're Happy and You Know It'.

The Rainbow Song

If it's raining and the sun is in the sky,
Put your umbrella down and look up high,
For a rainbow will be forming,
And the colours are so pleasing,
When it's raining and the sun is in the sky.

It is red and orange, yellow, green and blue,
And there's purple somewhere in the rainbow, too!
All the colours are so lovely,
And the stripes they are so curvy,
When it's raining and the sun is shining, too.

So if the weather isn't dry, do not despair,
For it might be that there is a rainbow there,
In the sky above your head,
Purple, yellow, green and red,
Blue and orange stripes appearing in the air.

Story sequencing for *How the Zebras Got Their Stripes*

Baboon sits by the river.

Gazelle and Antelope are hot and thirsty.
They go to the river to get a drink.

Baboon tells Gazelle and Antelope to go away.

Gazelle and Antelope tell Cheetah that
Baboon will not let them drink at the river.

Cheetah walks to the river to get a drink.

Baboon tells Cheetah to go away.

Cheetah tells the Zebras that
Baboon will not let anyone drink at the river.

The Zebras walk to the river.

Baboon tells the Zebras to go away.

The Zebras drink from the river.

Baboon chases the Zebras away.

Baboon and the Zebras get burnt by the campfire
and fall into the river.

The Zebras now have stripes and Baboon has burnt his bottom!

Story sequencing for *Why Anansi the Spider has Eight Thin Legs*

Anansi is hungry, but lunch is not ready yet.

Anansi's mum tells Anansi to tie a strand of web to the cooking pot, which she will tug when lunch is ready.

Anansi goes for a walk and sees Rabbit, who is boiling carrots.

Anansi ties a strand of web to Rabbit's pan of carrots.

Anansi walks again until he spots Chimp and Impala, who are chopping melon and grapes.

Anansi ties a strand of web to Chimp and Impala's salad bowl.

Anansi walks again until he sees Frog and Buffalo, who are cooking a stir-fry.

Anansi ties a strand of web to Frog and Buffalo's wok.

Anansi walks again until he spots Lizard and Mouse, who are cutting sandwiches into shapes.

Anansi ties a strand of web to Lizard and Mouse's plate.

Soon, Anansi has a strand of web tied to each of his eight legs.

Suddenly, all of the food is ready at once!

Anansi's legs are stretched and stretched until they are long and thin.

Story sequencing for *The Case of the Golden Trainer*

Inky, Snake and Bee are running in a race with their friend, Martin Speed.

The Fun Run Organiser welcomes everyone to the Fun Run.

Martin goes to the toilet before the race starts.

When it is time for the Fun Run to start, Martin is nowhere to be seen. The race has to start without him.

Helen Health crosses the finish line first.

Martin shouts for help. He has been locked in the toilet!

Detective Inky talks to the suspects.

Everyone tells Inky where they were before the race.

Helen Health tells Inky that she was getting some chocolate at the stall.

The stall owner says, "I cannot remember seeing Helen".

Helen fidgets and goes bright red.

Helen tells Inky that she locked Martin in the toilet because she wanted to win the race.

The Fun Run Organiser gives Martin the Golden Trainer.

Story sequencing for *The Case of the Vanishing Cakes*

Inky and Snake have come to see Bee take part in a Cake Contest at the Town Hall.

All of the cooks gather in the kitchen, and the Mayor explains the rules.

The cooks unpack their eggs and flour, and start mixing.

The Mayor walks around and talks to each cook.

Laila is going to make a lemon drizzle cake, which the Mayor does not like.

Soon, it is time for all of the cakes to be baked.

The cooks sit in the garden while their cakes are cooking. The Mayor slips away.

All of the cooks go back into the kitchen.

The cooks discover that all but one of the cakes have vanished!

Detective Inky looks for clues.

A trail of chocolate chips and raisins leads to the Mayor, who is covered in crumbs.

The Mayor confesses that he ate all of the cakes.

The Mayor cleans the kitchen while everyone else eats Laila's lemon drizzle cake.

Story sequencing for *The Un-Lucky Ring*

Megan is studying hard for her maths test
while Tom has a nap.

Dad says Megan should go for a walk.

Tom wants to go for a walk, too, and goes to get Mum.

Megan, Tom, Mum and Dad put on their boots
and go for a walk.

Tom spots a gold owl ring in the woods and picks it up.

Mum says, "The owl is made from gemstones. How lucky!"

It starts raining, and the family goes home.

On Monday morning, Tom lends Megan his owl ring
to bring her luck for her maths test.

Megan gets ten out of ten in her maths test. The ring is lucky!

Megan gives back Tom's owl ring
to bring him luck for his spelling test in the afternoon.

Tom clutches his owl ring, but the spelling test is very hard.

Tom gets every spelling wrong.

Tom's ring is not so lucky after all!

Story sequencing for *The Rainbow*

The different sorts of weather introduce themselves – all except the rainbow, who is very shy.

The rain and the sun have a disagreement about who should be in the sky.

The rain says that the flowers need a drink.

Then the sun says that the trees need some sunlight.

The wind and the snow are fed up of listening to the disagreement.

The wind says that the rain and the sun should share the sky.

The rain falls in big droplets and the sun shines brightly.

The flowers stop wilting and the trees start growing again.

The sunlight shines in the raindrops and makes colourful stripes in the sky. It is the rainbow!

All of the children point at the rainbow.

The rain and the sun never argue again.

Retelling the story: Comic strip template 1

Retelling the story: Comic strip template 2

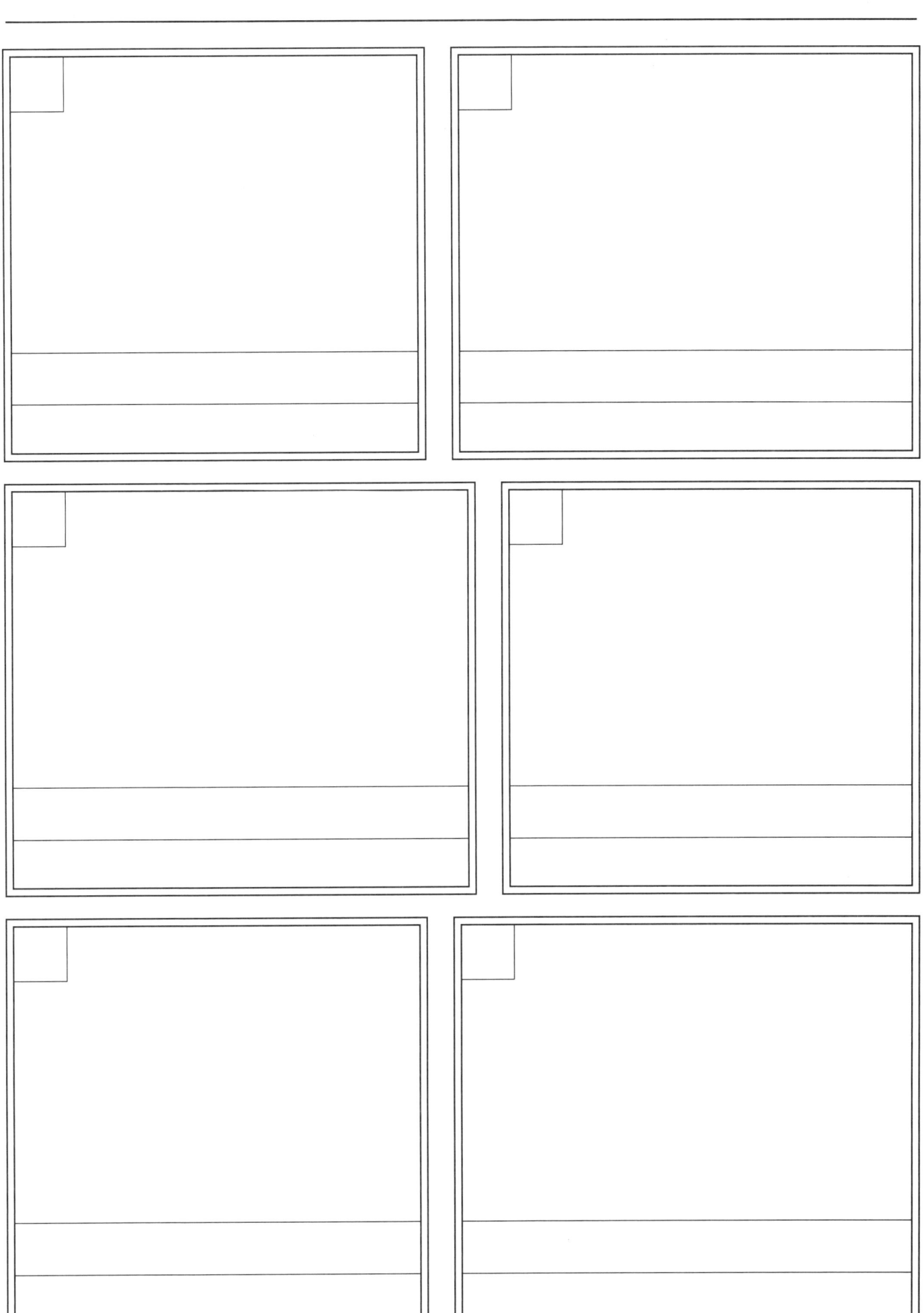

Looking at the characters

How the Zebras Got Their Stripes

1. Circle the adjectives that could be used to describe Baboon.

2. Underline the adjectives that could be used to describe the Zebras.

generous   friendly   mean   cruel
nice   horrible   grumpy   rude
hot   angry   brave
selfish   helpful   thirsty

3. Use some adjectives from the box to write sentences about Baboon and the Zebras.

_____
_____
_____
_____
_____

4. Which character would you like to be friends with? Why?

_____
_____
_____

5. Have you finished? Draw the Zebras on the back of this sheet.

Looking at the characters

Why Anansi the Spider has Eight Thin Legs

1. Circle the adjectives that could be used to describe Anansi.

2. Underline the adjectives that could be used to describe his friends.

> greedy   cruel   nice   happy
> friendly   angry   generous
> mean   hungry   practical
> rude   inventive   brave

3. Use some adjectives from the box to write sentences about Anansi and his friends.

_____
_____
_____
_____
_____

4. Read the sentences, and highlight the correct adjectives.

- Anansi whistles, hums, sings, grins and beams to himself. This means he is **happy** / **sad**.
- At the **beginning** of the play, Anansi's legs are **long and thin** / **short and stubby**.
- At the **end** of the play, Anansi's legs are **long and thin** / **short and stubby**.

5. Have you finished? Draw Anansi on the back of this sheet.

Looking at the characters

The Case of the Golden Trainer

1. Circle the adjectives that could be used to describe Helen Health.

nervous   mean   quick   helpful
selfish   clever   friendly
embarrassed
sheepish   slow
nice
generous   competitive

2. Use some adjectives from the box to write sentences about Helen Health.

_____
_____
_____
_____
_____

3. Martin Speed is described as being 'quick' and 'very good at running'. What other adjectives mean 'quick'? Write them in the box.

4. Have you finished? Draw Martin Speed on the back of this sheet.

Looking at the characters

The Case of the Vanishing Cakes

1. Circle the adjectives that could be used to describe the Mayor.

greedy   clever   good   helpful

mean   sneaky

nice   selfish   sad

sorry   dirty   bad

2. Use some adjectives from the box to write sentences about the Mayor.

_____
_____
_____
_____
_____
_____
_____

3. Who made marvellous, super-duper, scrummy chocolate cupcakes? _____

4. Who made blueberry muffins? _____

5. Who made the cake that the Mayor did **not** like? _____

6. Did Snake and Inky bake cakes? _____

7. Have you finished? Draw the Mayor on the back of this sheet.

Looking at the characters

The Un-Lucky Ring

1. Circle the adjectives that could be used to describe Megan.

2. Underline the adjectives that could be used to describe Tom.

> clever   nervous   eager   brave
>
> brainy   lucky   sleepy
>
> helpful
>
> angry   unlucky   good
>
> mean

3. Use some adjectives from the box to write sentences about Tom and Megan.

_____
_____
_____
_____
_____
_____
_____
_____

4. Who found the golden owl ring? _____

5. Is Tom nice to Megan when she is nervous? _____

6. Do Tom and Megan get on well? _____

7. Have you finished? Draw Tom and Megan on the back of this sheet.

Looking at the characters

The Rainbow

1. Read the adjectives in the box, and use them to complete the sentences underneath.

striped   freezing   strong   cold
colourful   damp
bright   cool
wet   light   hot
blustery

The **rain** is _____

The **snow** is _____

The **wind** is _____

The **sun** is _____

A **rainbow** is _____

2. Complete the sentences below.

Children fly kites when it is _____ .

_____ falls instead of rain when it is very cold.

The _____ heats up the ground.

The _____ and the _____ are needed to make a rainbow.

3. Have you finished? Draw the weather you like best on the back of this sheet.

Cross-curricular activities

Do a class project on animals (literacy, science, art and crafts)

After reading the plays *How the Zebras Got Their Stripes* and *Why Anansi the Spider has Eight Thin Legs,* encourage the children to find out more about the animals that appear in these plays.

- Split the children up into groups, ensuring that each group contains some more able children and some less able.
- Give each group an animal to research, or allow each group to choose its own animal.
- Look at nature books and websites with the children, and help them to find out as much as they can about their group's animal: for example, what it eats, how many legs it has, and what colour it is. More able children can be asked to find out, for example, how fast the animal can run, whether it lives in a big group or by itself, what countries or continents it can be found on, what kind of habitat it lives in, whether the animal is endangered or not, and what a group of the animals is called (for example, a group of zebras is called a herd). Encourage all of the children to write a sentence or two each about their group's animal. Each child in the group should write about a different aspect of the animal so that their sentences are not all the same.
- Help the children to find photographs of their group's animal, and provide art and craft materials so that they can each draw, paint or collage pictures of it. Make a display of the children's pictures with, for example, a herd of zebras in one corner and a flock of crows in another.
- Get each group of children to stand up and tell the rest of the class what they found out about their animal. In practice, this might just mean getting the children to read out the sentences they wrote about their animal.

Learn about myths, legends and folk tales (literacy, science)

Both *How the Zebras Got Their Stripes* and *Why Anansi the Spider has Eight Thin Legs* are based on traditional stories. Use these plays to expand the children's understanding of myths and legends.

- Explain that myths, legends and folk tales are very old stories that often try to explain how something came to be the way that it is.
- Remind the children that *How the Zebras Got Their Stripes* and *Why Anansi the Spider has Eight Thin Legs* both try to explain how certain animals came to look the way they do: zebras, with their stripes; baboons, with their bald, red bottoms; and spiders, with their eight long, thin legs.
- Explain that we still do not know for certain why these animals look the way they do. Scientists have suggested that a zebra's stripes help it to hide from other animals that want to eat it, or that the stripes make it difficult for flies to land on the zebra and bite it, or that the stripes help the zebra to keep warm in cold weather and cool in hot weather, but no one is sure. Encourage the children to think of other possible reasons for these animals looking the way they do.
- Read some more traditional stories, such as *The Three Billy Goats Gruff, Rumpelstiltskin, The Enormous Turnip* or *The Wind and the Sun* to the children.

Find out about camouflage (science, art and crafts)

After reading *How the Zebras Got Their Stripes,* help the children to learn that some animals have coloured or patterned skin that helps them to hide from other animals, and explain that this is called camouflage.

- Explain that there is more than one type of camouflage. Some animals have skin or fur that is the same colour as the place in which they live (for example, a polar bear in the Arctic snow); some animals have very patterned skin or fur, which makes it difficult to see their outlines clearly (for example, a leopard in a treetop); some animals have the ability to change the colour of their skin to match their backgrounds (for example, a chameleon or an octopus); some animals decorate themselves with plants or sand to hide in a particular place; and some animals have evolved over many years to look like something else (for example, a stick insect, which looks like a twig on the tree in which it lives).
- Show the children pictures of camouflaged animals.
- Provide the children with some animal stencils, pencils, scissors, and paper with different colours or patterns on it. Make sure that there are lots of different colours and patterns to choose from. Origami paper works well.
- Give each child two pieces of the same paper (or one large piece, which can be cut in half), and make sure that each child gets a different colour or pattern from the child next to him or her.
- Have each child draw the outline of an animal (or trace inside an animal stencil) onto the back of one piece of paper and cut it out, so as to make one animal and one matching background.
- Have the children place their animal shapes first onto paper that has the same pattern or colour, and then onto paper with a different colour or pattern. Ask the children where the animal stands out most.

Looking at different homes (art and crafts)

Before performing *Why Anansi the Spider has Eight Thin Legs,* research the different sorts of homes that people have around the world.

- Show the children examples of unusual types of homes, as well as the more common apartments, houses and bungalows.
- Together with the children, find out about the different materials used to build the homes as well as the different designs.
- Provide a large sheet of paper for each child in the class. The children each paint a picture of the kind of home they would like to have. The best five of these pictures can then be stuck to the wall behind the stage so as to form a little street when performing *Why Anansi the Spider has Eight Thin Legs.*

Make Anansi the spider (art and crafts)

After reading *Why Anansi the Spider has Eight Thin Legs,* have the children make some spiders of their own using air-drying clay or plasticine, pipe cleaners, paint and googly eyes or buttons.

- Each child takes a small ball of air-drying clay or plasticine, and rolls it out into a long, thin strip.
- They then take four pipe cleaners and twist them together at the middle to make eight legs.
- Once they are happy with their legs, they wrap the strip of clay (or plasticine) around the middle of the pipe cleaners (covering the twisted part completely) and smooth the clay back into a ball, to form the spider's body.
- Depending on the resources available, the children can either use a pencil to give their spiders some eyes, or they can push buttons or googly eyes into the clay.
- If using the air-drying clay, the children will have to leave the spiders to harden completely before painting them. If using the plasticine, the spiders are ready now.
- To finish off their spiders, the children should bend each of the pipe cleaner legs to give their spider some knees and feet.
- When the spiders are finished, the children can take them home and put them in the shower to scare their parents!

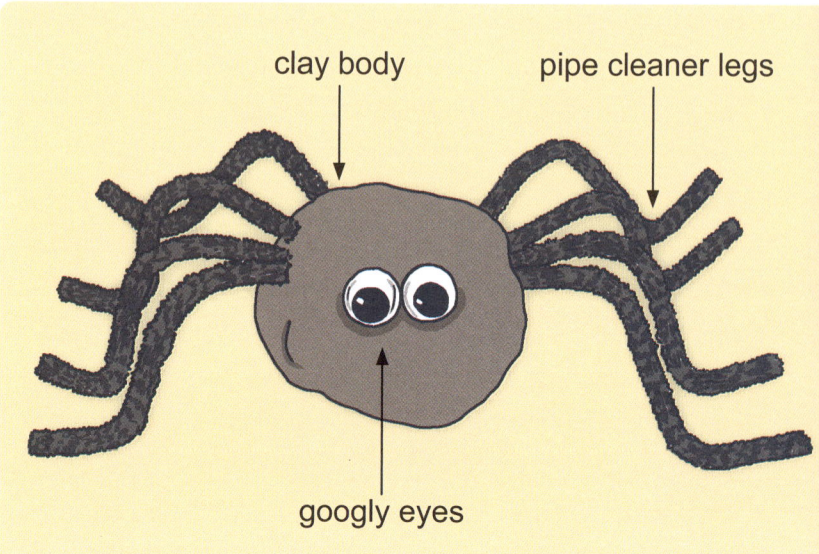

Have a fun run! (sports)

After reading *The Case of the Golden Trainer,* have a fun run at the school. Running not only helps with the children's physical health, but it can also help the children to think more clearly.

- Set a short running course around the school grounds: around 1.5 to 2 km is a good length for young children.
- Encourage the children to dress up in fancy dress for their fun run.
- Hand the golden trainer trophy to the first child to cross the finish line.

Bake a cake (cooking, maths)

After reading *The Case of the Vanishing Cakes,* teach the children how to bake a simple cake.

- Find a very simple recipe that can be completed in the time allotted for the lesson. Before doing this activity, it is important to find out if the children in the class have any allergies and to choose a recipe that avoids any known allergens.

- Make sure that the children understand what a healthy portion of cake looks like. In the play, the mayor had far too much cake, and this is not healthy!
- If the children's parents need to buy the ingredients, write the list of ingredients on the board and have the children copy the list and take it home. This provides additional handwriting practice.
- Encourage the children to weigh and measure out their own ingredients during the lesson. This is a good opportunity for the children to practise their maths skills. (If the parents are providing the ingredients, make sure they know not to measure out the right amount of each ingredient beforehand.)
- Use this activity as an opportunity to find out about carbon footprints, and to look at where each ingredient comes from and how it is produced.

Look at different types of tree (science, art and crafts)

Before performing *The Case of the Golden Trainer* or *The Un-Lucky Ring,* do some research about the different types of trees that grow in the local area.

- Ask the children to bring in fallen leaves for a leaf collection, and use the leaves to make leaf print pictures. Ask questions about the different types of leaf. Are they all the same shape? What colour are they? Are they rounded or pointed? How many lobes do they have?
- Encourage the more able children to use books or nature websites to try to identify the different types of tree from the different leaf shapes.
- Look at pictures of trees in books and, if possible, take the children for a walk around the school grounds – or around a local park or forest – and point out the various different types of tree.
- Plant a tree in the school grounds, and teach the children how to look after it.
- Provide large sheets of paper for the children and ask each child in the class to paint a different type of tree and write the name underneath. The best of these pictures can then be used as props in the plays: stick them to the wall behind the stage so as to form a park or a forest.

Find out about luck (literacy)

After reading *The Un-Lucky Ring,* discuss luck and superstitions with the children.

- Ask the children if they know what luck is, explaining the meaning if necessary. Then explain that a superstition is when people believe that doing (or not doing) something will bring them good (or bad) luck: for example, many people cross their fingers for good luck.
- Ask the children if they know of any other superstitions, such as breaking mirrors (said to be bad luck) or finding a four-leafed clover (for good luck).
- Some people have lucky objects, such as lucky socks that they wear for exams or running races. Ask the children if any of them have lucky objects.
- Help the children to use the internet or look in books to find out about luck and superstitions in other cultures.
- Draw two columns on the board: one for good luck and one for bad luck, and write up all of the superstitions that the children found out about.

Find out how rainbows are made (science)

After reading *The Rainbow,* make a rainbow in the classroom.

- Find out how rainbows are really made. How does this compare to the explanation given in the play? (It is broadly the same.)
- Make a rainbow by shining a torch through a prism and onto a sheet of white paper. Explain that the raindrops act like the prism and turn the sunlight into a rainbow.

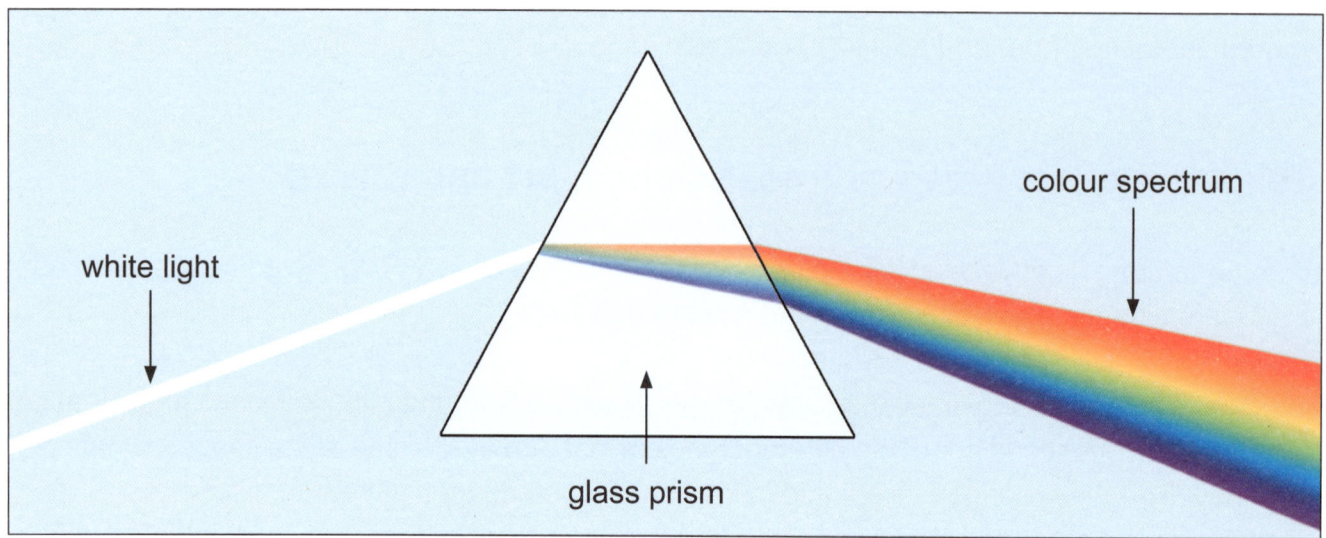

- Use the rainbow picture on page 111 and encourage the children to colour it in using the same colours they saw in the prism experiment. Make sure they put the colours in the right order: red, orange, yellow, green, blue, indigo, violet.
- Teach the children a song that helps them to remember the colours of the rainbow.

Find out about the weather (science)

Use *The Rainbow* as the starting point for a class project on the weather.

- Ask the children if they know the names of the seasons, and write them on the board.
- Then ask the children to think of the different sorts of weather we have in each season: for example, in Europe the children might suggest that it is hot and sunny in summer, foggy in autumn, cold and snowy in winter, and rainy in spring. While in south east Asia, the children might say that it is wet in the rainy season and sunny in the dry season.
- Write the weather words underneath the seasons on the board. Try to get the children to think of as many different weather words as possible.
- Provide a large piece of paper for each child. Show the children how to fold the paper in half and then in half again, so that when the paper is unfolded there are four equal sections. (If there children live in an area that has only two identifiable seasons, they should fold the paper once only to make two equal sections.) In each section, the children write the name of the season and one or two sentences to describe the weather in that season, with an illustration of the weather underneath.
- Help the children to learn about climate change, and what we can do to help our planet.

Find out about the water cycle (science)

Use *The Rainbow* as the starting point for a class project on the water cycle.

- Together with the children, look in books or at websites to help them find out as much as they can about the water cycle.
- Explain that water is always moving (or being moved) from seas and rivers, up to the clouds and back again in an endless cycle. Encourage the children to draw pictures of the water cycle, and annotate them with the following steps.

1. The sun shines on seas and rivers, and heats up the water.
2. The water evaporates (turns into little droplets, which float up into the sky).
3. The droplets condense (form clouds) in the sky.
4. The rain falls from the clouds.
5. The rain on the land forms rivers, which flow back down to the sea to be evaporated again.

Writing activities (literacy)

After reading any of the plays, the children can further explore the play's plot and characters with the following activities.

- The children each draw a picture of their favourite character, and write one or two sentences about why they like this particular character best.
- The children rewrite the plot of the play as a story in their own words. This activity will help the children to improve their comprehension as well as their writing skills.
- The children take another simple story that they know well, and rewrite it in the form of a play script. Good examples of very simple stories can be found in the Jolly Phonics Readers. It helps if the children choose a story that already contains a lot of dialogue. Encourage younger or less able children to re-enact one of the stories using toys or figures instead of rewriting it.

Mask and prop templates

The following pages provide reproducible mask and prop templates. Each template is clearly labelled with the character or prop name and the play(s) in which it appears.

Animal masks instructions

1. Photocopy each mask and stick onto thin card.
2. Find photographs of the animals, and encourage the children to colour in their animal masks using the right colours.
3. Cut out the masks (or get the children to cut them out).
4. Add elastic or string to the back, so that each mask fits a child's head comfortably.

Sandwich board instructions

1. For each sandwich board, take two large rectangles of sky blue card measuring roughly 420mm by 297mm (A3), or big enough to cover the torso of a child.
2. Make two small holes about a child's head width apart in the top of each rectangle of card.
3. Use ribbon or string to tie the two rectangles of card together, creating shoulder straps.
4. Make two copies of the cloud and two copies of the rain, snow, sun, rainbow or wind template.
5. Colour the weather pictures and cut them out.
6. Use the weather pictures to decorate the front and back of the sandwich board.

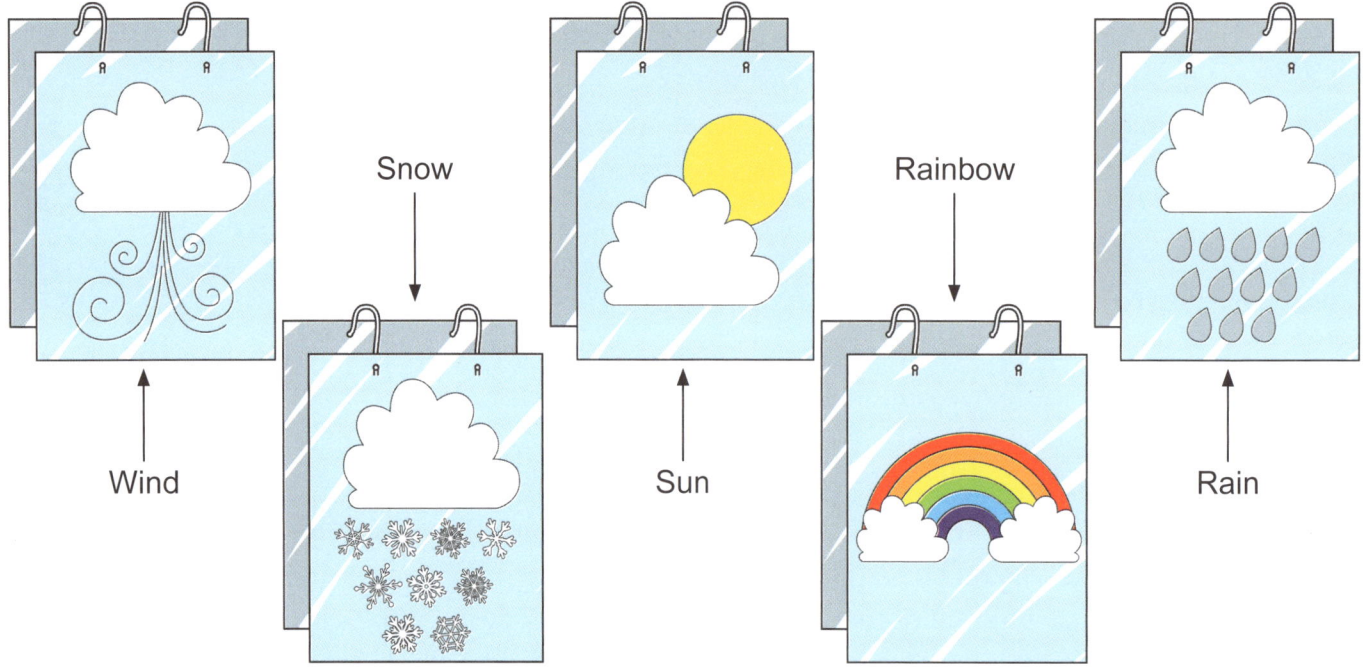

Wind · Snow · Sun · Rainbow · Rain

Baboon

How the Zebras Got Their Stripes

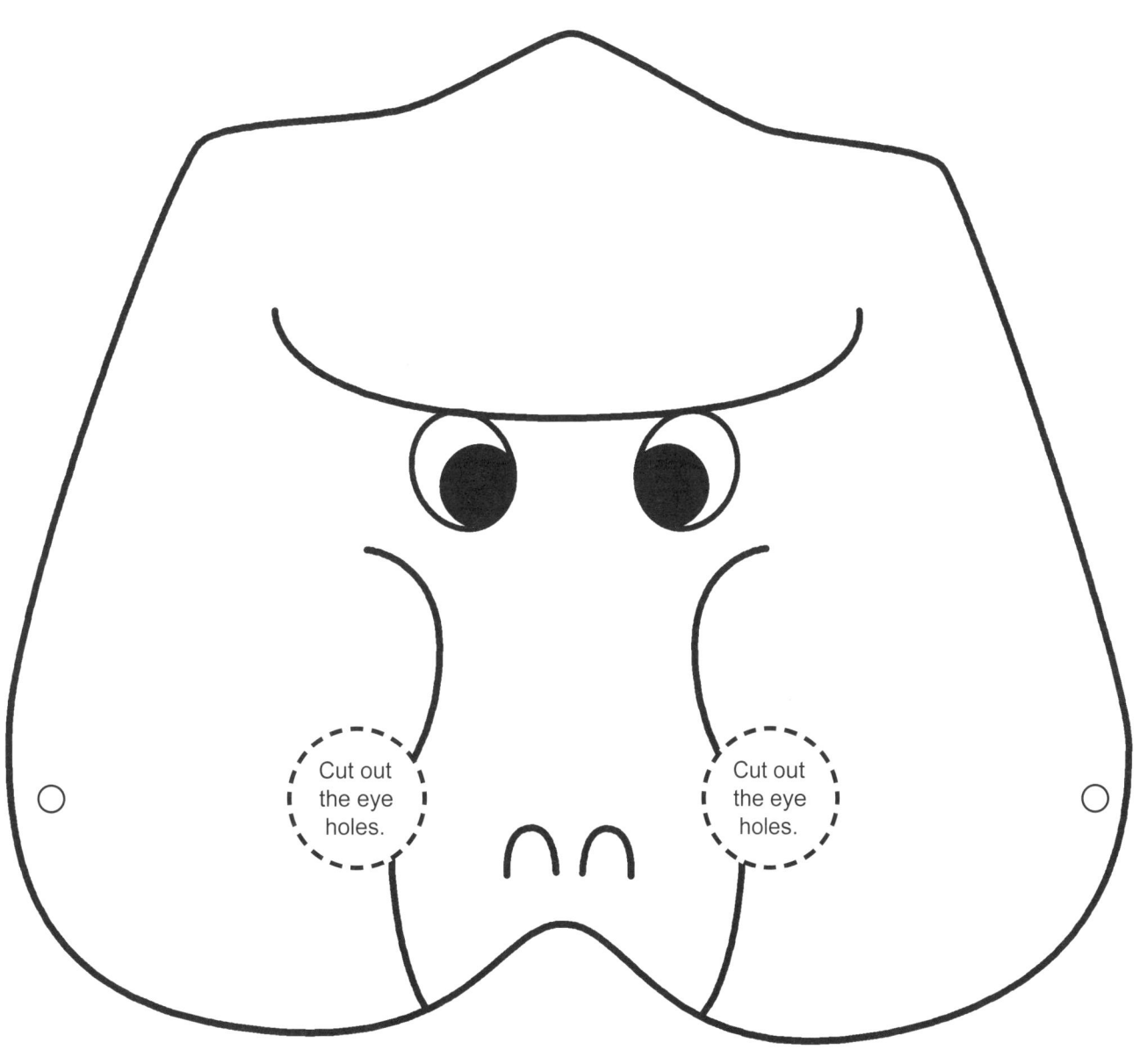

Crow

Both folk tales plays

Instructions

1. Photocopy this page and stick it onto thin card.
2. Colour both parts of the mask.
3. Cut out both parts of the mask.
4. Fold the beak in half along the centre line.
5. Fold down the two tabs on the beak and glue them to the face part of the mask.
6. Add elastic or string to the back, so that each mask fits a child's head comfortably.

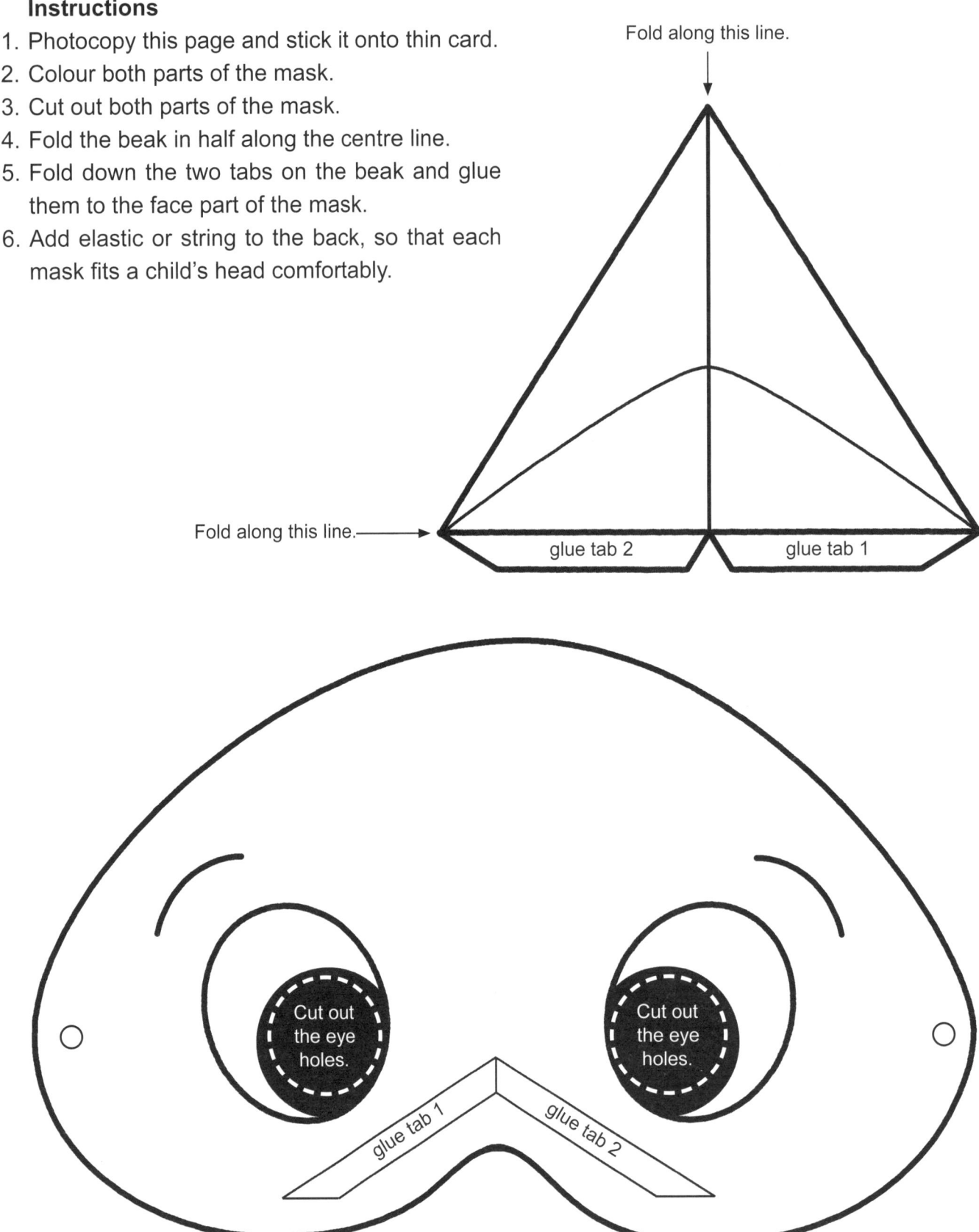

Mummy/Daddy/Little Zebra (white mask)

How the Zebras Got Their Stripes

Mummy/Daddy/Little Zebra (striped mask)

How the Zebras Got Their Stripes

Gazelle

How the Zebras Got Their Stripes

Antelope

How the Zebras Got Their Stripes

Cheetah

How the Zebras Got Their Stripes

Anansi/Mummy Spider

Why Anansi the Spider has Eight Thin Legs

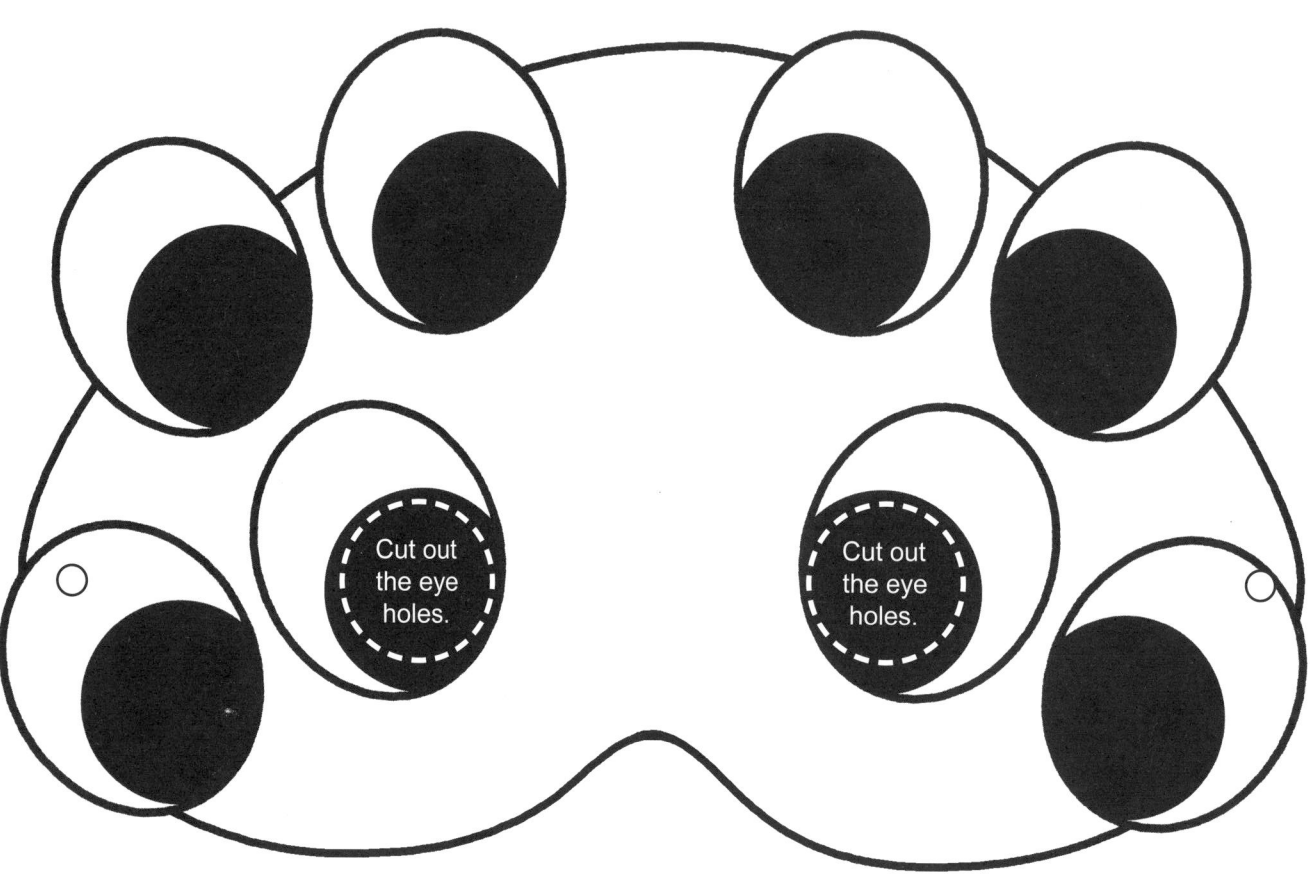

Rabbit

Why Anansi the Spider has Eight Thin Legs

Chimp

Why Anansi the Spider has Eight Thin Legs

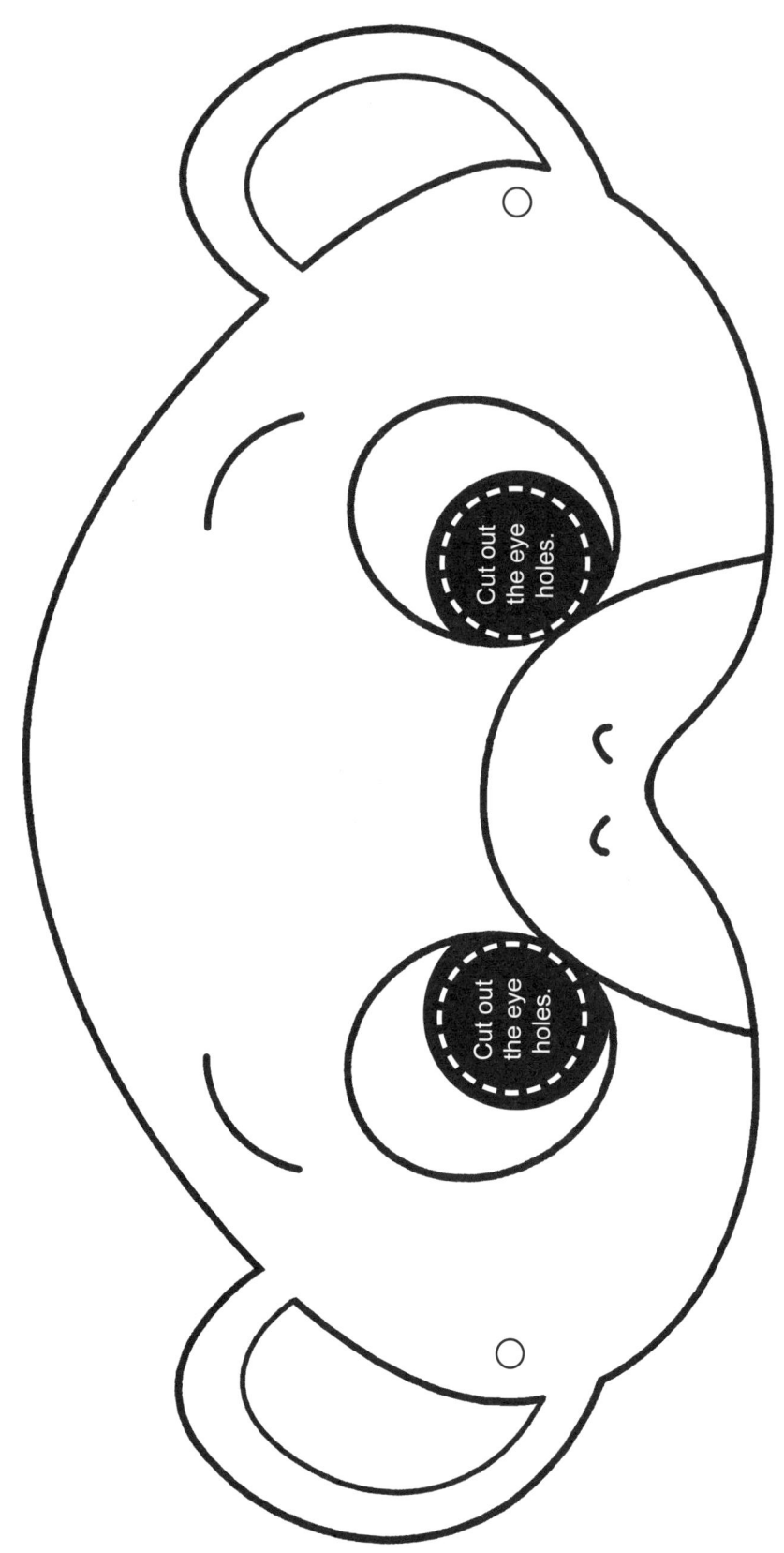

Buffalo
Why Anansi the Spider has Eight Thin Legs

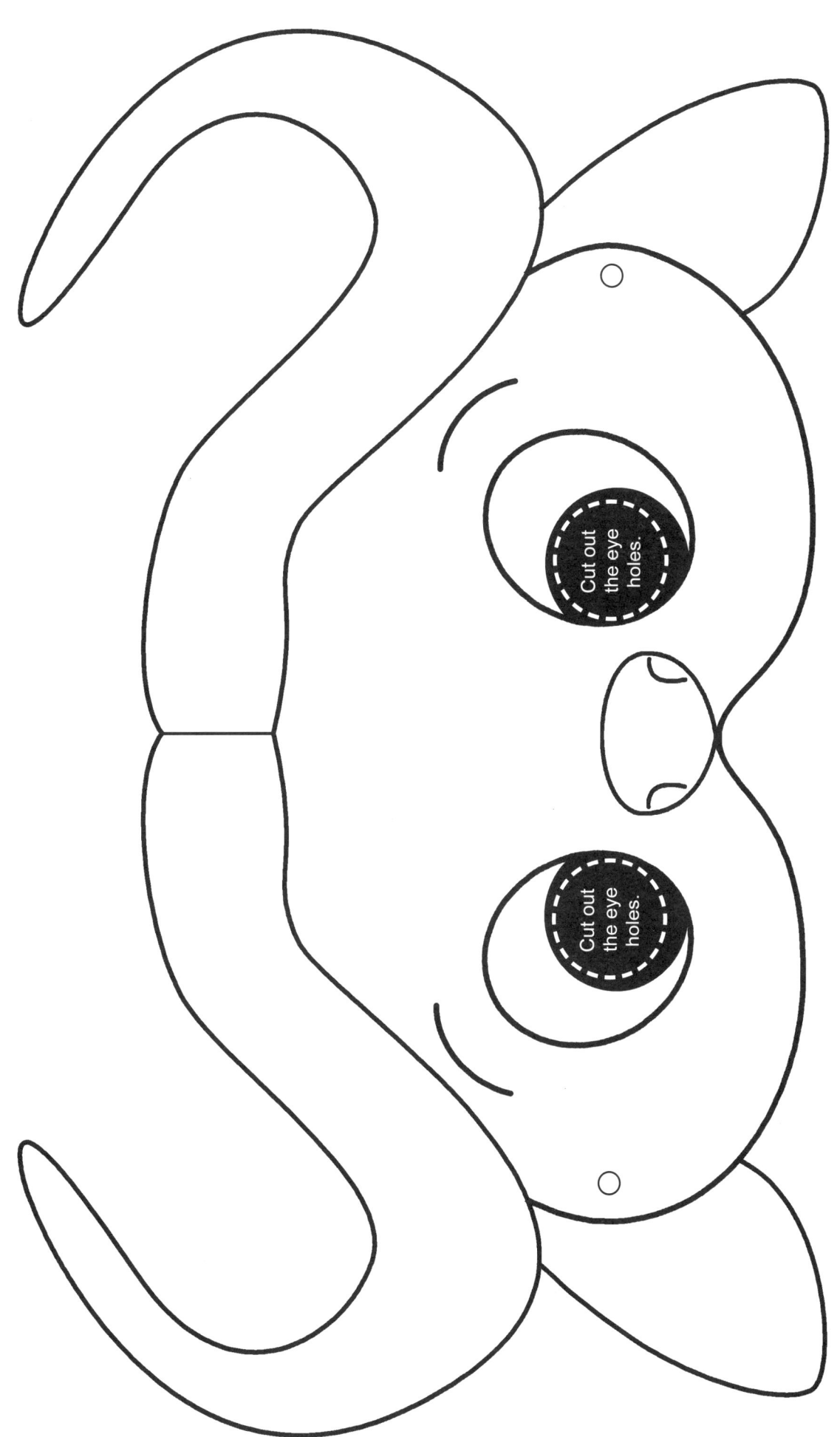

Impala

Why Anansi the Spider has Eight Thin Legs

Mouse

Why Anansi the Spider has Eight Thin Legs

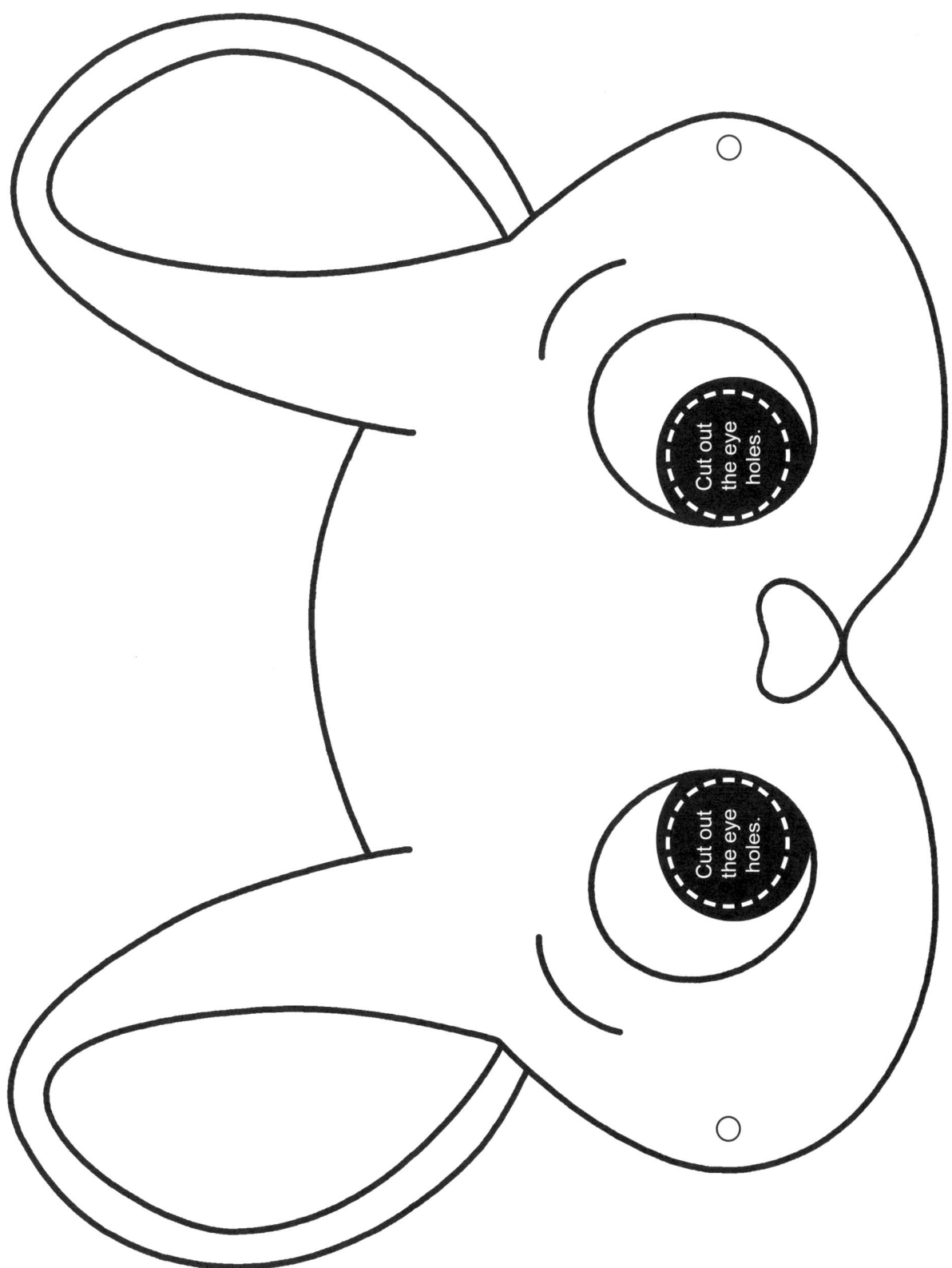

Frog

Why Anansi the Spider has Eight Thin Legs

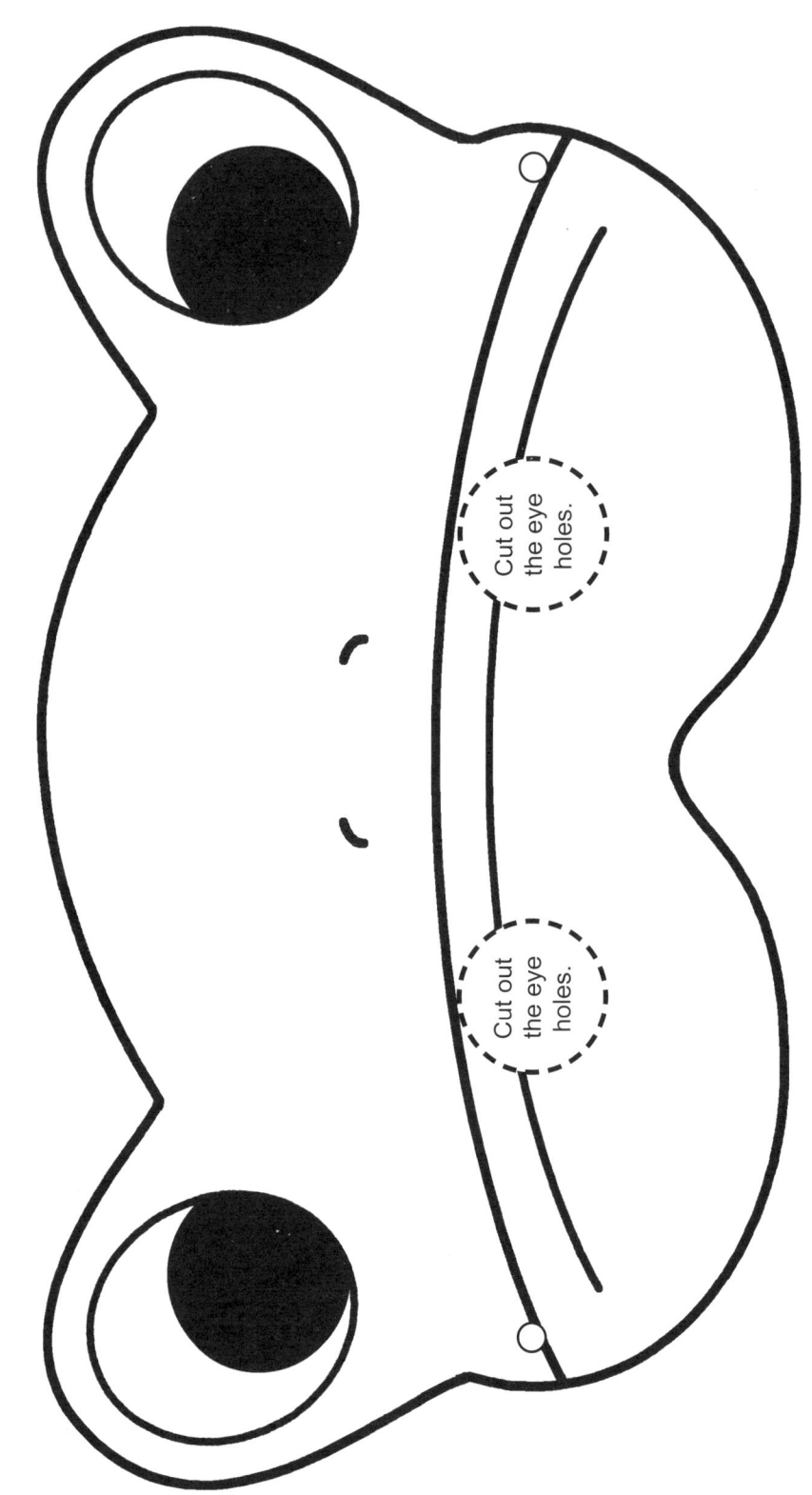

Lizard

Why Anansi the Spider has Eight Thin Legs

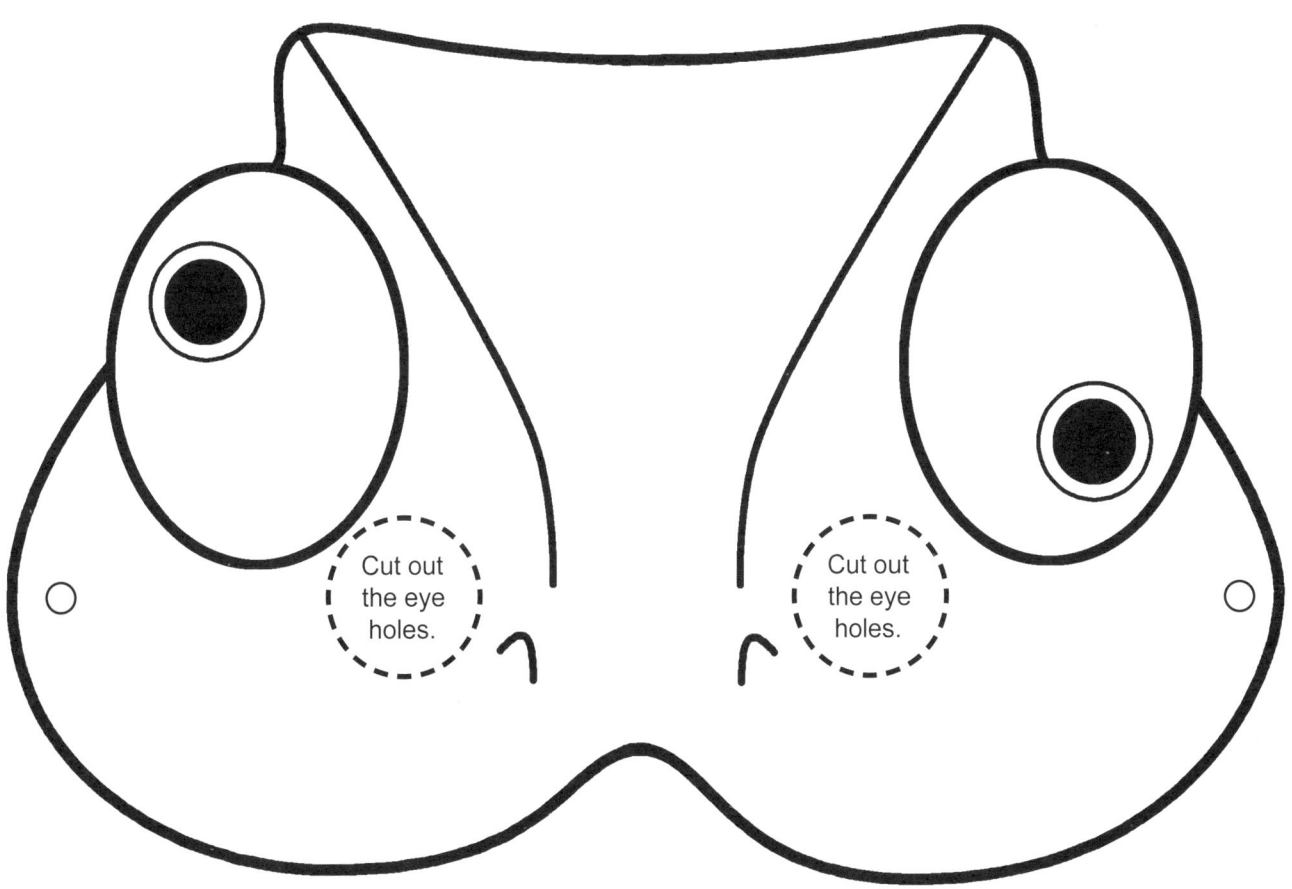

Inky

Both Inky Mouse investigates plays

Snake

Both Inky Mouse investigates plays

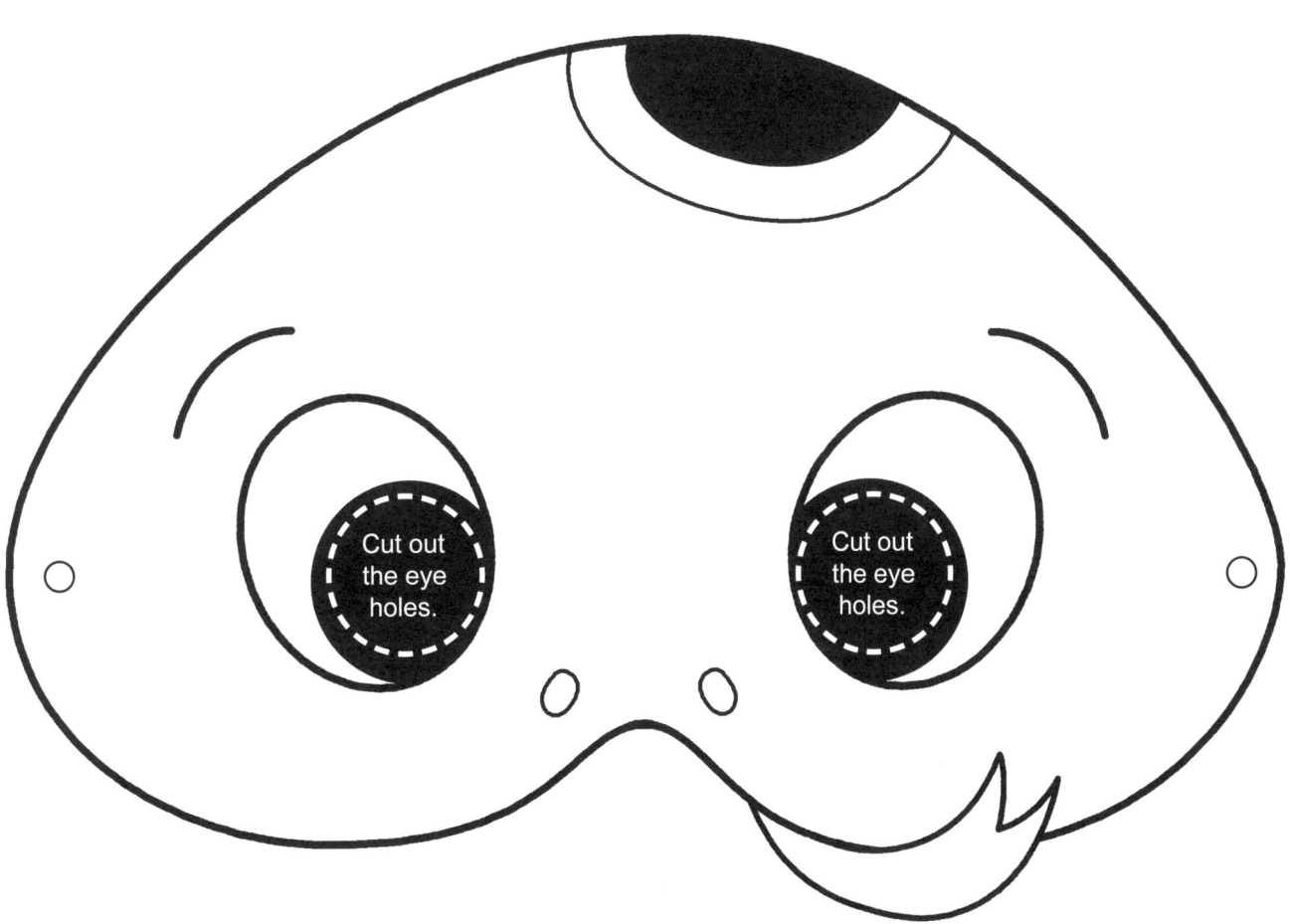

95

Bee

Both Inky Mouse investigates plays

Magnifying glass

Both Inky Mouse investigates plays

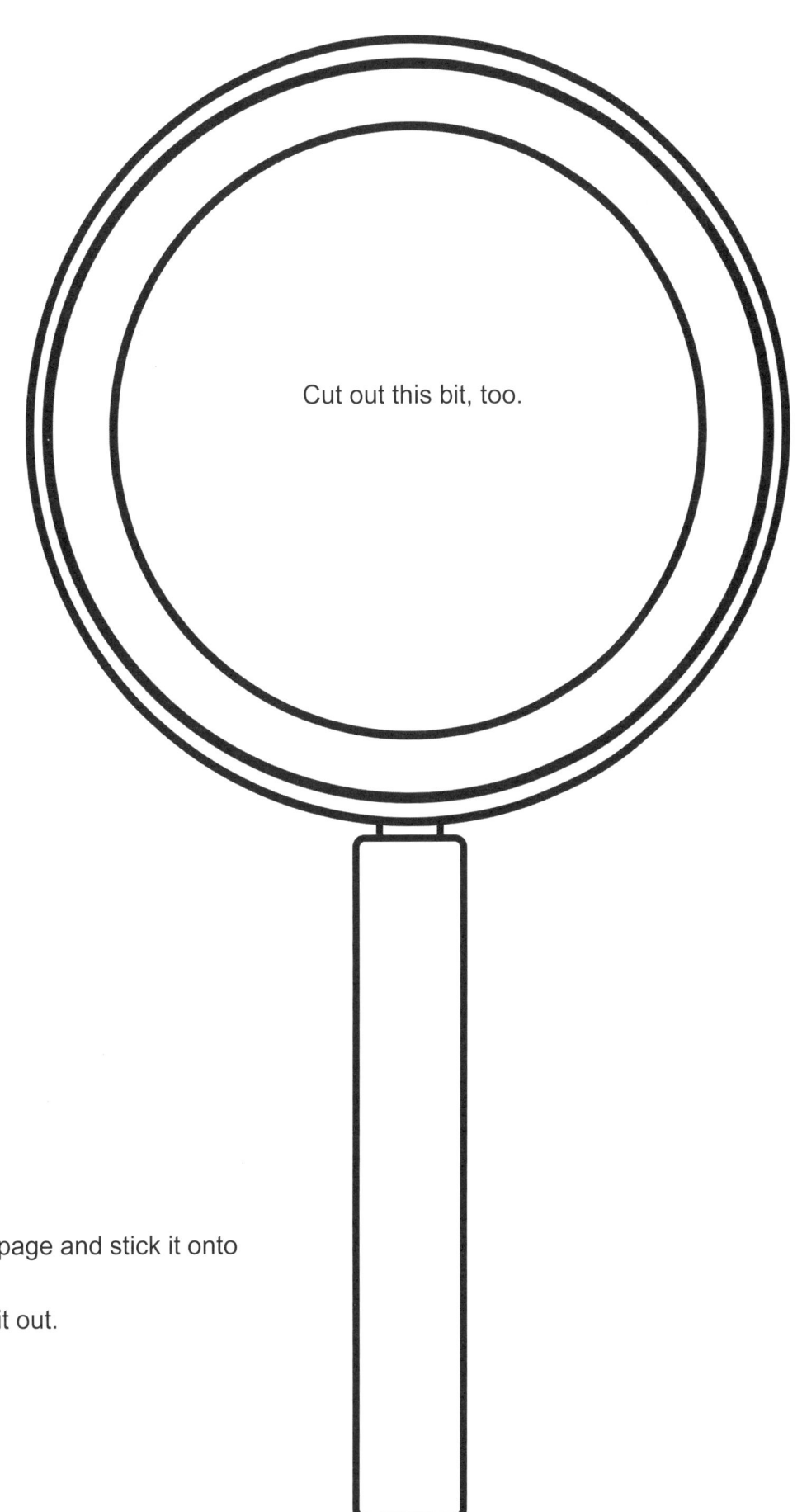

Cut out this bit, too.

Instructions
1. Photocopy this page and stick it onto thick card.
2. Colour and cut it out.

Campfire

How the Zebras Got Their Stripes

Instructions

1. Photocopy both pages and stick onto thick card.
2. Paint both parts on both sides, using red, yellow and orange for the flames.
3. When dry, cut out the flames and slot them together so that they stand up.
4. Stick on some red, yellow and orange tissue paper; then glue some twigs around the base.

Cut out this slot.

Golden Trainer trophy

Detective Inky in... The Case of the Golden Trainer

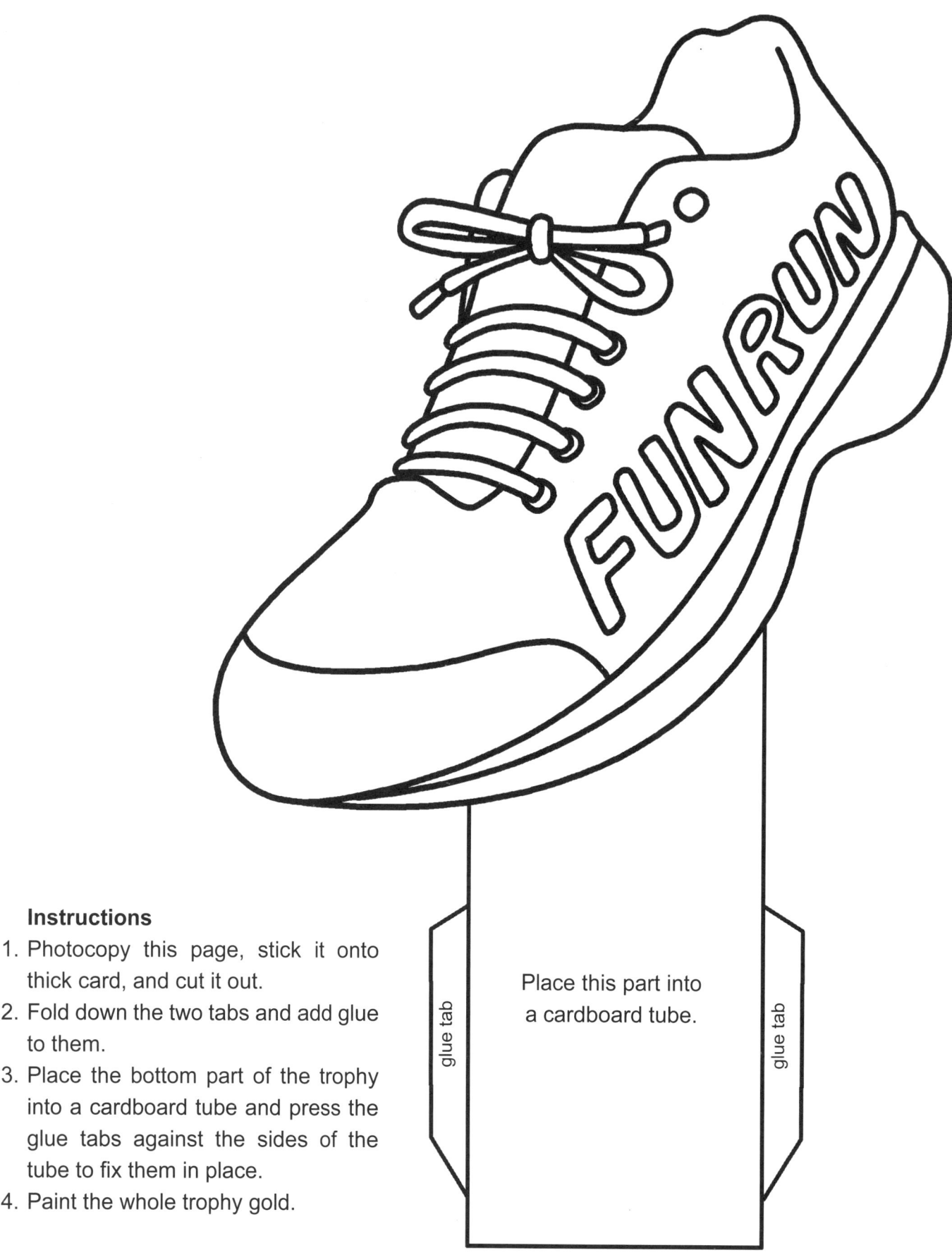

Instructions

1. Photocopy this page, stick it onto thick card, and cut it out.
2. Fold down the two tabs and add glue to them.
3. Place the bottom part of the trophy into a cardboard tube and press the glue tabs against the sides of the tube to fix them in place.
4. Paint the whole trophy gold.

Mayor's chains

Detective Inky in...The Case of the Vanishing Cakes

Instructions
1. Photocopy this page and glue it onto thin card.
2. Paint all of the parts gold on both sides, and cut them out.
3. Use a needle and thick thread to string the chains together.

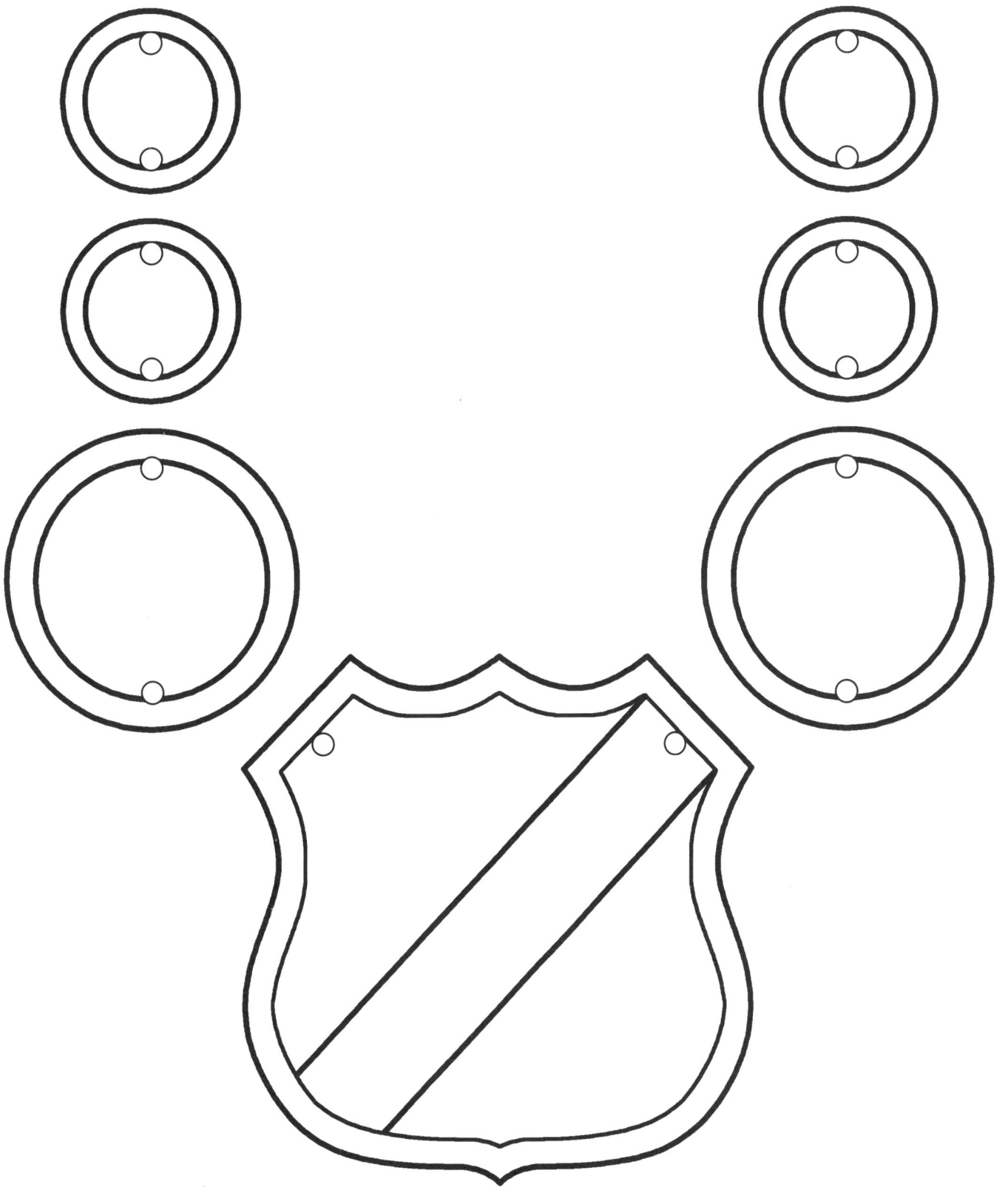

Flower pots

Detective Inky in...The Case of the Vanishing Cakes

Cut out this slot.

Instructions

1. Photocopy both pages and stick onto thick card.
2. Paint both parts on both sides.
3. When dry, cut out the flower pots and slot them together so that they stand up.

Golden owl ring

The Un-Lucky Ring

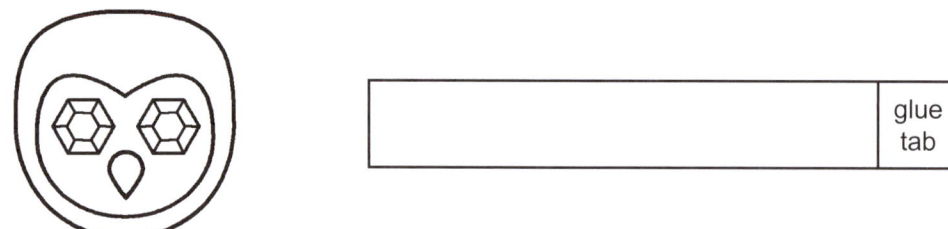

Instructions

1. Photocopy the image above, and glue it onto thin card.
2. Paint both parts gold on both sides, and cut them out.
3. Glue the two ends of the rectangle together to make a ring shape.
4. Paint the gemstone eyes a bright colour or, alternatively, glue plastic gemstones onto the eyes.
5. Glue the owl shape onto the ring.

Kite

The Rainbow

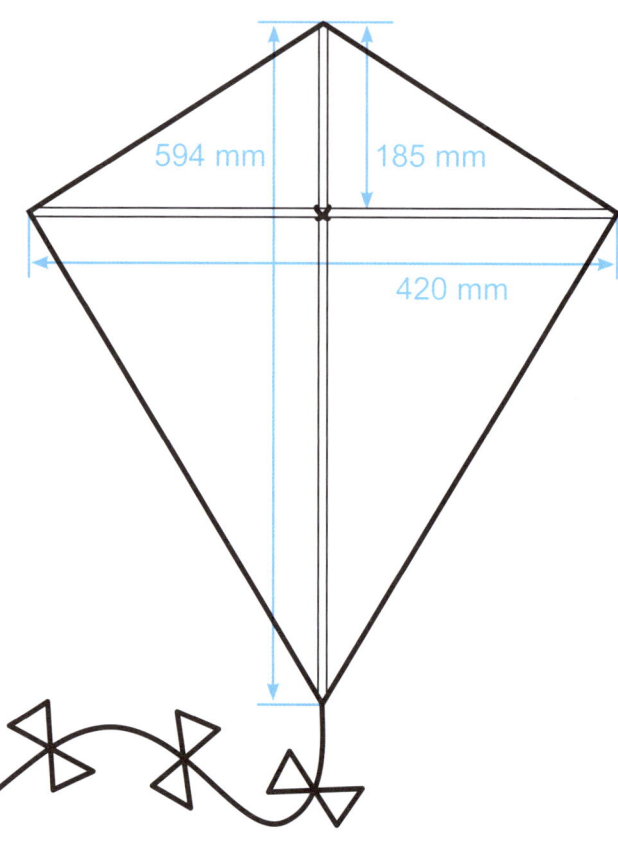

Instructions

1. Take a large piece of paper 420 mm by 594 mm (A2), and cut it into a kite shape according to the diagram opposite.
2. Take two narrow wooden rods, one 420 mm and one 594 mm. Form the rods into a cross shape, with the centre of the 420 mm rod 185 mm from one end of the 594 mm rod. Tie the rods together with string where they meet.
3. Tape the ends of the rod cross to the corners of the paper kite.
4. Tie another piece of string to the bottom of the kite to make a tail.
5. Add coloured paper bows to the tail.
6. Paint a bright, simple design on the front of the kite.

Leaves and flowers

The Rainbow

Instructions

1. Make several copies of this page and glue them onto thin card.
2. Paint on both sides, and cut out the leaves and flowers.
3. Glue a pipe cleaner to each leaf or flower.
4. Twist the pipe cleaners together to form bunches of leaves and flowers.

Sun

The Rainbow

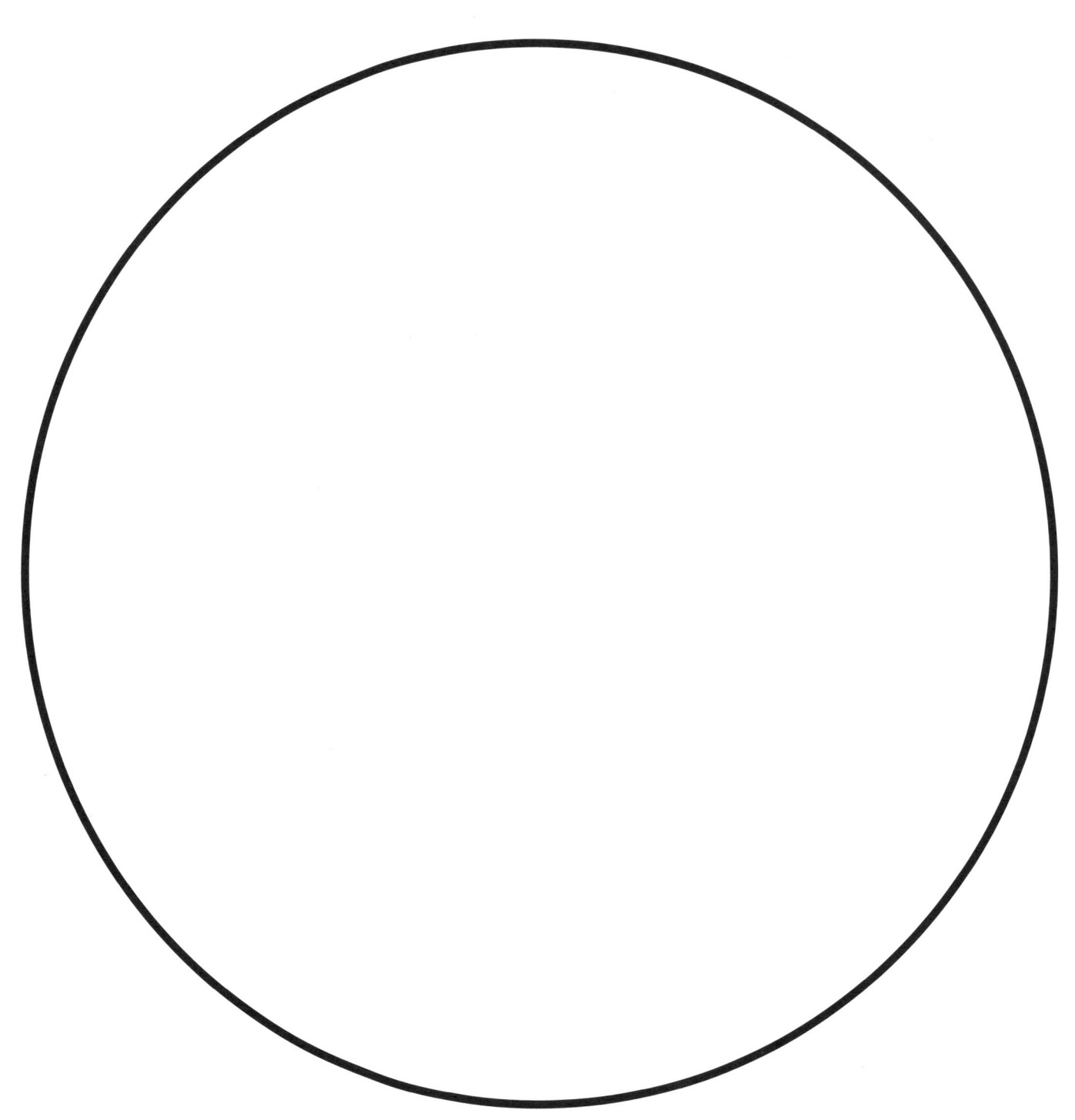

Cloud

The Rainbow

107

Rain

The Rainbow

Snow

The Rainbow

Wind

The Rainbow

Rainbow
The Rainbow

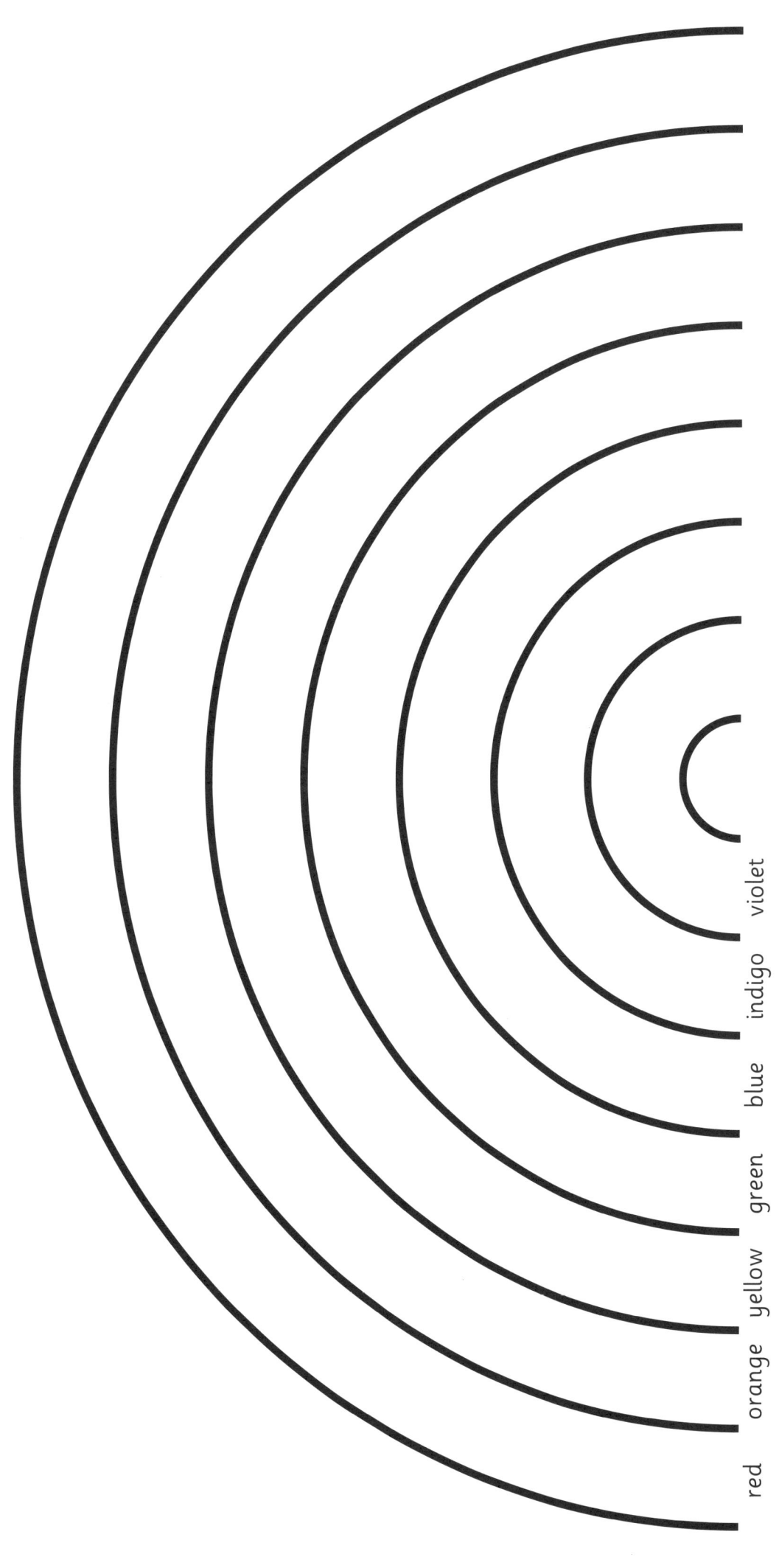

111

Small clouds

The Rainbow